This book takes you on a very perso
and faith! As these two battle cance~   ~~ p~~~~~~y ~~ ~~~ glory
of God. It is inspiring to see that through the struggle and pain, the will
of God was paramount in their hearts and minds. It is enlightening as
you follow the ups and downs of their saga that each had to find their
respective path - together - but separate. John was pursuing all that
he could yet get from life clear to the very end. Joy, on the other hand,
had to walk this road with him, with full awareness that she ultimately
would have to go on alone.

I found myself drawn into the intrigue of all the external trauma
and drama while a settled determination and peace prevailed through
it all. Words cannot do justice to the places this book will take you as
you go from the beginning to the blessed END.

Anita Paulsen

Joy takes you on her husband's unique cancer journey and fills it with
information, insight, humor, tenderness, love, and absolute confidence
in God's plan, regardless of the outcome. Her story will touch the lives
of all who read it, whether you have your own personal cancer journey
or travel this journey with a loved one. May God use Joy's words to
comfort, strengthen, and give peace!

Debbie Parks

EITHER WAY, IT'S OKAY

A Story of Faithfulness, Trust, and Determination to Face Cancer Together With an Eternal Perspective

Cynthia —
Oh those many years
ago when I was just
starting out — Thanks
for helping me — May some
words in this book speak
to your soul —
Love —
Joy

More books by Joy Bach

Life Moments with Joy
More Life Moments with Joy
The Challenge

EITHER WAY, IT'S OKAY

A Story of Faithfulness, Trust, and
Determination to Face Cancer Together
With an Eternal Perspective

JOY BACH

Paperback ISBN 978-0-9994956-5-0

Publishing Service Provided by

Orison Publishers, Inc.

PO Box 188, Grantham, PA 17027

www.OrisonPublishers.com

DEDICATION

God:
I am very aware this journey would have been a totally different kind of experience without God by our side. We continually felt His presence. The Bible speaks of a peace that is beyond understanding. That was God's gift to us.

John:
It was an honor to witness his humble spirit as he endured countless chemo and radiation sessions, hospitalizations, a multitude of doctor appointments and a handful of pills each day. As he lost his strength, he deteriorated to a cane, walker, wheelchair and finally the bed. But he never complained and managed to keep his sense of humor intact. His love and care for me remained evident until he was no longer coherent. His release from this world was bittersweet.

Family and Friends:
I treasure the memories of our village; always there to help. Some made sure we were fed while others took care of tasks that needed to be done around the house. We received an abundance of cards, texts, emails, and phone calls. We did not walk this journey alone.

Doctors:
He had numerous doctors who guided his journey; some with loving care and concern. A special thanks to Dr. Jose Ness who facilitated his journey with extra attention, even while he was on vacation.

"You saw me before I was born.
Every day of my life was recorded in your book.
Every moment was laid out before a single day had passed."
Psalm 139:16 (NLT)

CONTENTS

INTRODUCTION

There are moments in my life that will be embedded in my soul until the end of my days. One of those moments occurred during the summer of 2012, as I sat in my car in a restaurant parking lot. My cell phone vibrated, and I saw dad's name and phone number appear on the screen. Completely unprepared for what was to come next, I answered the call. After preliminary greetings had been exchanged, he was quiet for a moment before saying, "The doctor found something." I immediately knew what was meant by his statement. Cancer. The doctor had determined that malignant cancer had been discovered. Time seemed to stop as both of us processed the news. I began to cry. Dad's next words symbolically exemplified the perspective that would sustain our family during the journey ahead. "Your mom and I have peace about this," he quietly stated. "We are trusting in the Lord for the outcome, regardless of what that may be. Either way, it's ok."

As meticulously described within the content of these pages, life for mom and dad changed in many ways after dad's cancer diagnosis. In addition to managing a precise schedule for prescription medication, daily tasks often included appointments with various doctors who scheduled tests, procedures, and treatments. Although they were at times overwhelmed and exhausted, mom and dad's faith never wavered. The outcome of the situation was in God's hands, and they refused to surrender their sense of peace to the disquieting existence of despair and anguish. Instead, they held each other and trusted in the will of God.

As time passed, and treatment options were exhausted, we had to face the reality that dad's time was limited. As we prepared to say goodbye, I asked mom one day if she would ask dad to write me a letter before he died. In March 2015, during what would be our last visit, dad said he had a surprise for me. He had tried to write the letter, but each attempt was futile, as he couldn't convey in words how much he had loved being my dad, and what an honor it was to call me his daughter. Instead, he had decided to put words into action. He told me that he would be honored if I would allow him to legally adopt me. I was overwhelmed, as I had wanted him to adopt me since I was twelve years old. Unrestrained tears coursed down our cheeks as we embraced. As a little girl, I couldn't have imagined such an act of unselfish love from a father, and my soul cried out in gratitude as a multitude of emotions washed over me. After being my dad for almost forty years, I was officially adopted by John Bach on March 26, 2015. I am incredibly thankful to be his daughter and will always treasure the memory of my adoption.

May 22, 2015, as I prepared report cards on the last Friday of the school year, my mind was immersed in a sea of memories as I thought about the impending end of my father's earthly life. Pensively, I leaned back in my chair and closed my eyes, contemplating the reality of what was to come. An incoming call on my cell phone suspended my reverie, and I took a deep breath when I saw mom's number on the screen, mentally preparing myself for the possibility that this was the call I had been expecting for days. When I answered the phone, I was surprised to hear dad's quivery voice as he struggled to formulate a greeting. Because he was so weak, mom held the phone to his ear while he talked. "I have a word for you," he whispered, his voice trembling. "Your word is daughter. I'm blessed to be your dad. I love you." Tears rolled down my cheeks as we said goodbye, and I offered a silent prayer of thankfulness for the profound impact of his carefully chosen word. I was his daughter. He was proud to be my dad. Waves of emotion enveloped me, and as I reflected upon the journey leading up to that final phone call, my heart overflowed with gratitude for the man who had become my father.

On May 26, 2015, two months after my adoption day, and four days after the final phone call, dad took his last breath and was welcomed into heaven to spend eternity with Jesus. Although I miss him every day and grieve his passing, I will always be grateful for the gift of my dad. To be chosen as a daughter is truly a wonderful gift.

Mom, I am incredibly proud of the way in which you lovingly documented dad's journey, as well as your own, within the pages of this book. Many people will be profoundly impacted by the testimony of your faithful trust in God, and your unshakeable determination, strength, and resilience during some of the most challenging days of your life. I am honored to be your daughter.

Lorri Bach
November 2022

PROLOGUE

A man of few words, the plastic surgeon quietly snipped on John's stitches where he had removed a growth. We were awaiting the result of the biopsy.

As the doctor worked, John asked, "So can you tell me the outcome of the test?"

"We'll talk about that in a minute."

Finally, he finished and allowed John to sit up. As he talked, he used medical terms we didn't understand. But we did recognize the word oncologist. We needed the result in English.

We traveled to our doctor, who had received the preliminary report and used words we understood like cancer, chemo and radiation.

We exited that doctor's office and held each other in the parking lot. John whispered in my ear, "Are you okay?" As amazing as it was to me, I answered, "Yes." When I asked him the same question, his response matched mine.

Standing in that parking lot, we were bathed in an overwhelming sense of peace. This was not an assurance that John would be healed, but the peace of knowing God would take care of us either way.

Our journey had begun.

CHAPTER ONE

My husband, John, owned a sleek, silver BMW R1150 RT, which he coddled like fine china. So why did he suddenly feel an urgent need for a second motorcycle? Peer pressure? Mid-life crisis in his 60's? One look at my face conveyed to him my bewilderment. No problem. He could explain all my questions away. His face lit up as he enlightened me with the details. "The 1150 is designed to ride on the slab." (Motorcycle language for highway). "That can get boring." The pitch of his voice elevated as his emotions took over. "It's time for some adventure. The one I want, a BMW F650 GS, is designed for off-road. Can't wait to get it."

Bless his heart. How could I say no?

As with any new toy, there were added expenditures. I was already well versed in the procurement of farkles. Let me explain. A farkle is a deemed necessary (in the mind of the farkler) modification to a motorcycle. But for John, this time there existed an even bigger need; how to ride off-road. That would involve instruction.

A four-day training was offered beginning April 13, 2012 on the other side of the state. John planned, eagerly awaited and occasionally feared what would be involved. The brochure stated "Riding sessions to challenge your mind allowing your bike to do things you never thought you could do. Expect achy bodies." Various techniques such as riding in ruts, sand, gravel, over large rocks and even railroad ties were included in the agenda. Sounded swell.

We had a group of friends John called his Starbucks Gang. This eclectic group of people met on a daily basis to discuss almost everything except politics. The gathering included health care workers, laborers, business owners, lawyers, professional office workers, farmers and retired. Since I don't like coffee, I only joined them on weekends, but he went daily; every morning before work and then again at 3:00 if he could make it. The Saturday after he got his new motorcycle, he rode it to Starbucks to show it off; I drove. As we sat at the table with our friends, someone yelled across to him, "Hey, John, you got a new motorcycle. What did Joy get?"

"She gets peace and quiet." He knew me well.

The big day arrived. He and three friends would meet and leave for the training from Starbucks. Just in case we might be late, we arrived there two hours early. Before they climbed on their bikes, I was asked to pray. With a kiss and hug he was on his way.

Phone calls kept me informed of his progress.

"I've fallen a few times. It's okay. Everyone is."

The next day the report was similar. More falling as they were taught how to ride over large rocks. But on the third day the phone call was different.

"I'm coming home. Dean will be accompanying me. We'll be there this afternoon."

No mention of why he was coming home early. Upon my arrival from work, I found him asleep in bed. He roused when I walked in.

"Are you okay?"

"I'm really tired. Just let me sleep."

Since he was diabetic, I asked if he had eaten.

"I'm too tired."

He slept all night, shivering under the covers. Concern niggled in the back of my mind. *I'm sure his blood sugar is off. How do I make a grown man test his blood sugars and eat? I don't.* More concerns when he awoke and climbed from bed. He walked with a limp.

"Oh, it's okay. I just landed on a large rock with my left hip when I fell once."

That didn't explain the swollen right foot.

"Well, one fall the bike landed on my foot and I had to have help to push it off."

Of course he did.

"John, you really need to check your sugars. I'm going to work, but please let me know how you are doing." Later that morning I received a phone call.

"I'm really hungry. Did I eat anything last night?"

Duh.

He limped and moaned his way through the day. I shortened my workday and became part caretaker. He was more comfortable in the big chair in the TV room than in bed. He wore sweatpants and a hooded sweatshirt with the hood pulled over his head, plus covered completely with a heavy fleece blanket, yet still shivered. I was digging deep to find any empathy for these self-inflicted wounds. However, that little voice in the back of my mind was whispering "This is more than just some bumps and bruises. He needs a doctor."

"John, I think you need to be seen by a doctor. I believe there's something else going on."

His response, in typical John fashion, "I'm okay. It will just take a few days to get better."

An email from a friend inquired, "How are you doing? I heard you had a little fun. Hope all is well."

Response: "Walking a little slow with a bruised hip on the left and a twisted ankle on the right, but worth every pain. I learned a lot."

The next day, when he called me at work, I knew the situation had changed. John would never voluntarily call a doctor.

"I've called Dr. Markle and have an appointment at 10:00."

The voice in my head talked louder. "See, I told you he wasn't okay." I left work to meet him at the doctor. When I arrived, John was sitting in his car in the parking lot. I walked toward him, but he yelled across to me through his open car window, "You need to get me a wheelchair. I don't think I can walk that far."

Those words traveled through my whole body. *He can't walk that far? Wheelchair? How had we come to this? God, I need you to give me courage and peace as I deal with what's going on.*

A novice at pushing a wheelchair, it's a wonder I didn't injure him further. I wanted answers now and ran into the door in my haste to get to the doctor. My concern for John overrode any humor in my reckless driving. With the advent of John's phone call that morning, I had also decided now was the time to have the doctor look at an unusual growth on John's neck. I hadn't been able to convince him to seek medical attention for it. Since I already had him at the doctor, this would be a good opportunity.

As we waited, John mentioned, "I hope he can help me with this pain in my hip."

"What about your foot? The doctor needs to see that too." We glanced at it, resting on the foot plate of the wheelchair, very visible since John was wearing shorts. Yep. It was still swollen. Being smashed by a motorcycle caused issues. "Okay, I'll mention both of them."

Concerned about the foot and hip, the doctor was ready to send John for X-rays when I said, "Please look at the lump on his neck. In the past few days, it's been growing."

As he examined it, he began to ask John questions.

"How long have you had this?'

"A year or two, but just recently it began to stick out."

"Why didn't you have it looked at?"

"I did. I went to a dermatologist about a year ago. He said it was okay."

"How long has it been protruding like this?

"It doesn't bulge all the time. Maybe about a week. It comes and goes."

"That's not good. It would be better if it stayed the same. You need to go to a specialist and have it looked at."

Before we left the doctor's office, we had an appointment with a plastic surgeon and orders for X-rays to be taken of John's hip and foot. As the nurse pushed the wheelchair to the parking lot, John pointed out his car. Astonished, the nurse asked, "You mean you drove here?"

Of course he did.

In tandem, we drove to the clinic where X-rays were to be taken. Leaving John in his car, I walked to the front desk, handed them the instructions from the doctor and requested a wheelchair for my husband.

"What are we X-raying today?"

"Left hip and right foot."

"That's unusual. When there's an accident, the injuries are usually on the same side. How did it happen?"

"Two motorcycle accidents."

"Oh."

Once again, I watched as my husband was pushed in a wheelchair by a nurse. My mind could not make that sight register. Events were happening too fast for me to keep up.

X-rays were taken and he was wheeled back to his car. I helped him in, but when I turned to go to my car, he said, "I'm going to need a cane to be able to walk. We need to stop and buy me one." *A cane? For my husband?* We stopped at a store, he stayed in the car and I carried a selection out for his decision. One was purchased. He went home and I returned to work.

No longer did we sleep in the bed. His hip would burn with pain. So, he slept in the big chair in the TV room. And he slept a lot. He tried going to work for a few hours…came home and slept for a few hours…and returned to work. In the evening he fell asleep by 6:00 and slept until bedtime. Since the chair was his bed, there was barely an interruption. I slept on the loveseat next to him. We had gained a new bedroom.

Good news from the X-rays. No fractures. It would just take time to heal.

CHAPTER TWO

I rode with John to his appointment to have the growth on his neck examined by Dr. Monteilh, the plastic surgeon recommended by Dr. Markle. John had progressed from wheelchair to cane, so we held hands as we entered this unfamiliar territory. After a brief assessment, the doctor, a man of few words, declared surgery was needed to remove the growth and scheduled it for April 25th.

John received a text from a friend: "How is your hip?"

John: "Still need a cane."

Lynn: "Sorry to hear you are hurting bad enough to need a cane. Just know I'm a phone call away. Praying for you."

Not only was John dealing with injuries and a growth, but he was losing weight. He had, over the past few months, deliberately lost down to his desired goal weight. But he hadn't stopped there. In a matter of days, he had lost six more pounds. Having been careful about what he ate as he dieted, he now ate and ate and still lost. I kept my concerns to myself, but spoke often with God. *Please give the doctor guidance and wisdom as he analyzes the reports. Something is wrong with my beloved. I'm so grateful I have You to turn to.*

Surgery was performed in the doctor's office. I stood by John's side as the doctor poked and prodded on his neck, then drew a circle around the area he planned to excise. He began to cut and cut, deeper and deeper. Apparently, the circle had not been large enough. By the time he was through creating the incision, the hole had doubled in size. I watched as the doctor carefully removed a strange looking growth that resembled a rather large oyster, complete with the ruffled, uneven edges. *Oh, that doesn't look okay.*

After lots of internal stitches, it was time to cauterize the bleeding. My eyes observed the blood loss with no reaction, but the smell of burning flesh assaulted my olfactory senses. Quickly, I stepped outside the room to breathe some clean air. When I returned, the external stitches had been completed and John was released to come back in a week for the test results.

Even with all that was going on with his body, John continued to push himself to work. As the owner of Design Dental Lab, he was an integral part of the business. But now his body exhibited a new symptom. He became covered with a rash; prickly and itching. Nights were unending as he tried to get comfortable in his chair. Good thing I'm a short person, as it seemed the loveseat was a semi-permanent arrangement.

We were part of a small group that met weekly through our church, but we chose to skip it, requesting prayer for our situation. Church was no longer attended and even though John had signed up for the Men's Getaway, he canceled his registration for that too. Rest was what John's body needed to be able to mend. We existed in a world of work and home.

I drove from work to meet John at Dr. Monteilh's office on May 2nd. Arriving before he did, I was walking toward the front door when I heard a car honking. It was John driving into the parking lot. I walked to meet him, and he handed me the last of a chocolate dipped ice cream cone from McDonald's.

"Here, I saved the last for you."

As I looked at the cone, I thought *this may be the last time I enjoy an ice cream cone like this. Depending on what the doctor tells us when we walk in there, we may walk out different people.* We entered the office, but before we could even sit down, John's name was called. I sucked the ice cream out of the unfinished cone and threw it away.

As the doctor snipped on the stitches, John asked, "So can you tell me the results of the test?"

"We'll talk about that in a minute."

My heart did a little lurch. If the results were okay, couldn't he just say, "Everything looks fine?" My pulse rate increased.

Finally, with John sitting on the examining table, the doctor began to talk.

"The preliminary report shows lymphatic tissue. We'll have to wait for the detailed pathology report to know just to what extent it has progressed."

What did that mean?

Even though John tried to get a clearer answer, the doctor continued to talk in medical terms. But he used a word we did understand, oncologist. He suggested we make an appointment next week to see Dr. Markle.

There was an elephant in the room, one not being mentioned, but filling all my spaces.

I had to stop at the front desk to pay the bill, which was an insult to my emotions as I just wanted to be with John. I exited the front door to find him waiting for me on the sidewalk. I walked straight into his arms. But nothing was really clear. The next morning, we entered Dr. Markle's office. We knew he had received the preliminary report and would clarify our situation for us. "The growth is malignant. You have cancer."

The elephant had been identified.

As the doctor talked, words like chemo and radiation bounced around in my brain. This would be an unfamiliar journey for us. The doctor explained due to John's diabetes, he would still be the point person in charge of that. But John would need to see an expert for a lymph node on his neck that needed to be removed. As we discussed possible doctors, I asked about our choices.

"The Cancer Center has several very good doctors. You won't be assigned just one doctor specific to you. If you want to deal with the same doctor every time, I recommend Dr. Jose Ness. He is very good." The option of having the same doctor every time sounded like the best fit for us.

We left Dr. Markle's office and stood on the sidewalk. Silently our arms encircled each other as we processed the words we had just heard. Then John whispered in my ear, "Are you okay?" Amazingly I answered, "Yes. Are you?" "Yes."

We had been bathed in an overwhelming sense of peace. We hadn't been given an assurance that John would be fine, but the peace of knowing that either way, it was okay. Jesus was right there in that parking lot and would travel through this uncharted territory with us.

In preparation for this odyssey, I created a binder displaying on the front and back a beautiful picture of Italy with the Mediterranean Sea in the distance. I chose that image to remind us of the day we stood and viewed that same panorama. Beneath the picture were the words **John's Cancer Journey, Diagnosed May 2, 2012.** I placed blank ruled filler paper on the three rings, pondering the words that would be declared there. *How would this journey end?*

Our pastor and wife, Phil and Anita, were also our friends and had been praying about the diagnosis. Instead of just a phone call to share our news, we took them to lunch. In his very matter-of-fact way, John explained the journey on which we were now embarking. Their concern was evident in their expressions of love. They would be there for us.

That evening John said, "Joy, I think we need to tell your boss about this. It will probably affect your work schedule. Can you text him and see if we can walk over?" "Of course, I will." And I did. But John never knew what I said that day as I took my phone from my pocket to communicate with my employer.

"Howard, are you home this evening? John and I would like to come by for a minute. He wants to disclose his diagnosis to you. He has no idea I told you the same day we found out. So put on your acting hat. I'm counting on you."

Yes, they were home and yes, we could come by. Since they lived in the neighborhood, it was just a matter of minutes before we were ushered onto their patio and offered a beverage. Once again John laid out the path before us. Kudos to Howard. He allowed John the honor of giving the details with no indication he already knew.

CHAPTER THREE

Our initial visit with Dr. Ness was on May 14, 2012. A smiling bundle of energy entered the room, hand extended toward John and then me. *So this is the man who will walk with us through this uncharted territory. I think I like him.*

Dr. Ness spied the binder and with a grin said, "I see you'll be taking notes. That's very good."

John immediately took over the conversation.

"I just want you to know I am someone who likes to accomplish things, to ride motorcycles and run a business. If this gets to the place where end of life decisions have to be made, I don't want any last-ditch efforts."

I wonder what Dr. Ness thinks of that? He handled it very well, as he sat on a stool and rolled to face John. With his ever-present smile, he said, "Well, let's not get ahead of ourselves. First, we need to know exactly what we are dealing with. We will make decisions as we go."

Again, John felt the need to express even more.

"You think you're in charge, but you're not. God is."

Bless Dr. Ness. He took it all in stride.

"We need to do further tests. There are many types of T-cells and this is a fairly complex issue. We need to send samples to another pathology lab at the University of Washington and it will take a week or two to get the results. Certain kinds are potentially fast growing. It seems you have the variety that is in the skin. That's the reason for your rash. We will do a CT of your neck, chest and belly looking for any more abnormal lumps. Then a PET scan for the growth of cells. That will determine if it is fast or slow growing. Next will be a bone marrow biopsy. We will be looking to see what stage you are in."

Taking notes as fast as I could, I was already on overload.

Dr. Ness continued. "If possible, I will want to start treatment two weeks from now. We'll do a blood draw today. Come back and see me in ten days."

Just that quickly it was over. At the front desk, appointments were scheduled; a follow-up with the doctor on the 25th at 10:15 and a bone marrow biopsy on the 30th at 3:00. As the elevator descended, John and I discussed Dr. Ness. We agreed, we liked him a lot.

John received a text from Paul Null, a pastor friend who lived in Oregon. "Any medical news yet? Still praying for my brother and sister. May I rest in the luxury of Bachville on Wednesday?"

"Still waiting for scheduling of tests and we would love to have you as our guest."

And life went on.

After the follow-up with Dr. Ness on the 25th, we drove to Spokane to have lunch with some very close friends, Moe and Sandi. We wanted to tell them the news in person. As we talked and then went to lunch, John seemed to have more energy, an encouraging sign. His days of excessive chilling appeared to be over.

The PET scan was scheduled for May 29th. We were told it would take two to three hours and he would not be allowed to drive home. When we arrived, they checked his blood sugar. It was 193. Their protocol was to cancel anything over 150. The radiologist was called, who spoke with John. "That's what my blood sugar runs historically. I don't see it going any lower." Since the chances of it getting better were slim, they decided to go ahead. A PET/CT were performed at the same time, without contrast. John's kidney function was already compromised, due to his diabetes. We were told contrast would do further damage.

The procedure exhausted him. I drove home and he headed straight to his chair/bed and slept all afternoon. As the evening progressed, John awoke refreshed and declared, "I think I can sleep in the bed tonight." After forty nights of utilizing the chair in the TV room, we held hands as we walked to the comfort of our bed. Lots of snuggling and spooning occurred.

The appointments just kept on coming. At 1:30 the next day, we arrived at Dr. Ness's office for the bone marrow biopsy. He directed John to climb on a table and motioned for me to leave the room. I asked to stay. He said no.

"Okay, tell me why I have to leave."

"I don't want to have to pick you up off the floor."

"I already watched more than one YouTube video of this process and know what to expect."

He let me stay.

I stood by the table and held John's hand while they used a chisel and hammer (or whatever they are called) to make a hole in his spine. Then a rather large needle was inserted to draw the marrow out, and a bandage was placed over the opening. We were released to go home with a final word from Dr. Ness. "I'll have the results in about a week."

On the 6th of June we returned to Dr. Ness's office. It was becoming a familiar place. We now knew the names of the employees and they knew ours. We were among friends.

"I have not received the pathology report from the University of Washington. The results of the bone marrow biopsy show no cancer, so it has not reached Stage 4. The PET scan reveals that the bulging lymph node is in Stage 2. I don't think it needs to be removed. Other nodes were discovered; two enlarged ones on the left portion of the neck and three nodules on the upper left neck. Your brain and liver are cancer free."

I breathed a sigh of relief.

He continued, "You have skin T-cell lymphoma. There are two kinds. You have primary aplastic lymphoma; skin involvement is aplastic. When it is mostly in skin it is like a chronic disease and will need light therapy or radiation. Chemotherapy is not a must, if this is the final diagnosis. It is unusual enough that it needs specialized service. I recommend Dr. Eileen Smith of Walla Walla for the skin issues. That's her specialty. We'll call you with an appointment for when you need to come back to see me. I'll know more then."

But as we all stood to leave the room John had one more request. "I have a motorcycle rally planned this weekend. Any reason why I can't go?"

With a grin on his face, Dr. Ness approved the trip.

John's strength had returned. A ride on his new motorcycle was just the medicine he needed, but halfway there the bike stopped working.

In disbelief his riding buddies gathered around. They tried all that they knew. A phone call was placed to the nearest motorcycle shop. A flat-bed truck from Spokane came to pick up him and the motorcycle. His friends traveled on without him. Within 24 hours it was fixed, being told it had something to do with the fuel not pumping correctly. John hopped on and made it to the last day of the rally.

Next, it was time for him to have his initial exam at the North-west Cancer Clinic. This was a fairly new building across the parking lot from our lab. We had observed the construction. A giant hole had been excavated, the dirt removed had been sifted and then utilized in making a barrier around the crater. Next, very thick concrete walls were poured. Upon inquiry, we had been told that was all necessary because radiation would be happening in that area of the final struc-ture. Little did we know John would be partaking of that. Dr. Sheila Rege now had her very own divider page in my binder.

The very next weekend was our annual Father's Day motorcycle rally in John Day, Oregon. John rode with his buddies around curve af-ter curve. I drove my sports car and stayed on the highway, which was much straighter and allowed me to go faster. I became known as the mule. If our friends needed me to take their tents, coolers, tarps, etc., we would meet that morning before we headed out and they would load it into my car. I made sure there was still a space for me to see out the back window.

I arrived before they did, so I claimed a spot for about twenty-five tents. We would all camp in the same area. Soon they arrived, tents were set up and they were discussing where to eat, when John said, "Joy, I have a problem. I don't have enough of my diabetes medicine." Big problem. Friday afternoon. Dr. Markle's service was called. It took some time, but the doctor called a prescription to Len's Drug Store in John Day and they filled it for us.

The fairgrounds filled with tents and six hundred people. Dooley Mountain was always a must on John's schedule. Located in eastern Oregon, the twisties beckoned him and his friends. When I say twist-ies, I mean lots of them. One hundred seventy curves on a fifteen-mile stretch. I, on the other hand, sat in my lawn chair and read, then gathered my crocheting and moved to the women's restroom where there were some couches, and I could charge my phone. I worked the yarn and looked forward to eating at Outpost, my favorite restaurant in town. My mouth already watered thinking of the Mexican pizza I planned to enjoy.

It was all good.

Sunday morning arrived quickly. My car was loaded and ready. We gathered for prayer and goodbyes. Then the sound of motorcycles being started filled the air; with one exception. John's wouldn't start.

Friends and many unknowns gathered around his motorcycle with varying ideas of what he needed to do. Nothing worked. A phone call was placed to the closest motorcycle shop which was in Boise, Idaho. That left me with a dilemma. John would have to ride with me. Where? My car was stuffed. Various smaller items were parceled out for the friends to take on their motorcycles. But it would be a cramped three and a half hour drive back home.

As John stood and looked at his non-functioning motorcycle, buddies were astonished at how cool and collected he seemed. It became a topic of conversation, and they even questioned him as to his laid-back attitude. He didn't give them the real answer. His diagnosis was being kept quiet, to prevent his business clientele from finding out yet. But I knew. Having a motorcycle that didn't work was nothing in comparison to having cancer. And he was still experiencing the peace that passes understanding.

All was well with his soul.

CHAPTER FOUR

For many years, my daughters and I met every two years to spend a week together in some beautiful place, staying in a timeshare one of them owned. Some of the more popular places required a reservation a year ahead of time. We had a trip planned for June 22nd to June 29th at Lake Tahoe. With John's blessing I flew to Reno, Nevada and they met me at the airport. It was a much-needed break for me, and we had a wonderful time.

While I was out of town, John had a check-up appointment with Dr. Ness. Arrangements were made to consult with a lymphoma specialist at the Seattle Cancer Care Alliance. We would be given the details later.

Sunday, July 8th, we had been asked to speak to the church about our journey. John was an old hand at speaking, giving seminars regularly around the country. I, on the other hand, had attended Toastmasters for years to get over my terror. I stood beside him on the platform, so very grateful I was able to share my part of the story. I could feel the growing boldness within me as we journeyed. As he spoke, John shared a verse that had become his motto: "For me to live is Christ and to die is gain. (Philippians 1:21 NIV) I want you all to know that either way is okay. I can be healed here or in heaven."

That afternoon, John received a text: "Just heard about your diagnosis. I'll be praying for you. Let me know what the doctors say." John: "Sorry I didn't get to tell you before today. Things aren't as bad as they sound though. They think it's something chronic, not life-threatening. I will know more tomorrow."

The next morning we drove to Seattle to consult with a specialist. Our new doctor's name was Andrei R. Shustov (from Ukraine). He was associated with the Fred Hutchinson Cancer Research Center. He was very friendly and shook our hands, then introduced us to a lady who accompanied him; Dr. Montgomery who was a Fellow at the Center.

Dr. Shustov got right to the analysis of John's situation.

"You have anaplastic large T-cell lymphoma. There are two varieties. Our primary diagnosis is that it is in your skin. The prognosis for the course of this type of cancer is seven to ten years. Chemo doesn't work with it. You will need radiation. The remission rate is very high; 93%. Then in three to five years you will need more radiation and will go into remission again. Each time it recurs we will zap it.

If it's systemic the outcome is 50/50. Some do well. We would use more aggressive chemo. Half of the patients relapse in the first year. It can be cured with chemo plus radiation. You have the ALK1 gene, which is a good thing. It really makes no difference in the early stages but may later. Before we go any further, we need to know what is in the lymph node, so we need a biopsy. The rash on your body is bizarre. We also need a biopsy of your skin."

Dr. Monteilh's contact information was given to Dr. Montgomery so she could request the results of the node biopsy.

"Again, it depends on if it's systemic or not. We will start with three or four cycles of chemo with three weeks in between and then radiation five days a week for four weeks. In six weeks you will have another PET scan. These treatments can be done in the TriCities. The variety you have is very rare, with only one to two percent of the people in the world developing it. There is a consortium researching this kind. The database is gathered in Milan, Italy. May we put you on the registry?"

John replied "Yes". I asked, "Does that mean we will get to go to Milan?"

With not even a smile, he just responded no. Then he spoke to the subject at hand. "Your first plan of action is to get an immediate appointment with the dermatologist in Walla Walla. She needs to do a punch biopsy."

The requested information from Dr. Monteilh had not yet arrived so we were dismissed to walk around the waterfront while we waited for them to call us back in. We held hands and talked, feeling overwhelmed. Yet we knew God was in charge of all of this. We could trust Him.

When we were called back, Dr. Shustov had the information he needed.

"Dr. Monteilh removed a deep skin lesion. That means you have the skin type, not systemic. The lymph node needs to be removed. When it is, Dr. Ness will receive the report first and then send it to me at SCAA."

We walked to our car deep in thought. As we drove out of the garage, we discussed our situation. We were in agreement. We had placed this journey in God's hands. We were taking care of our end and He would take care of His. We had an evening to enjoy in Seattle and so we did.

John felt the need to visit the Apple store and see all the new gadgets available. Within minutes my eyes glazed over, but we stayed an hour. After enjoying a delicious meal, we decided to walk to the waterfront. With frequent touching and holding of hands, we headed out. But John's feet became so painful we had to hail a taxi. Before going to the doctor's office, we had checked in at the timeshare provided by our daughter. It was ready and welcoming when we returned. We would be refreshed for our drive home in the morning.

A little side note here. When we got home, John proceeded to go online to Apple and order a new Mac. Was I surprised? No.

And now a new doctor's name was entered into my binder, Dr. Fong. His specialty was Otolaryngology, head and neck surgery. July 16th, we sat in his office as he explained his role in our journey. The node he was to remove was an external jugular node. I didn't care much for the word jugular, which sounded dangerous to me. Then he explained he might have to go deeper to find the source of the issue. That sounded even worse.

"You will be under anesthesia and monitored continually. The preliminary pathology will be done while you are still there. It will take about an hour. It will be outpatient, same day surgery. If you are taking aspirin, stop taking it NOW. You need to withhold it for a week before surgery. Excessive bleeding is a possibility. And on the day of surgery do not take any of your meds."

Surgery was scheduled for July 23rd. And yes, John had a regimen of one aspirin a day due to his atrial fibrillation. I was discovering each step involved choices that affected other areas. The aspirin was to prevent clotting due to his irregular heart rhythm. One more aspect to give to God as we learned the process of relinquishment.

The very next day we headed to Walla Walla for his appointment with Dr. Smith. Two new doctors in two days. She was very cordial, and I liked her immediately. The standard gown was handed to John and he was directed to remove all but his underwear. Believe me, she did a very thorough search.

"You have Eczema Craquele affecting your hands, feet and back. It's just what the word sounds like. Your skin is cracking. It is accompanied by extreme itching. I see where huge patches of your skin have fallen off. When it is on your feet, it makes walking painful. This is a skin issue related to lymphoma. One percent of people have this. In my twenty years of practice, I've seen one other case. You can use Cortisone four times a day, but if it gets better stop using it. I will want to re-assess in two weeks."

While I was processing that, she continued.

"Treating the skin is designed to make us happy. It doesn't fix the problem. You can use olive oil for the cracks. Every day place your hands and feet in water for twenty minutes to soften the skin and then put on white cotton gloves. After your shower, I recommend Cerave for your entire body. At bedtime, rub Aquaphor on your hands before you put on the gloves. Hands and feet take a long time; many months. I don't believe I need to do a biopsy."

During the 45-minute drive home, we talked about the newest development. This issue of cracking skin was causing problems at work. John held precision instruments all day, carving teeth. Some of the cracks were very deep, especially around his fingernails. And Aquaphor, recommended for his hands, would make it too slippery to be able to hold the equipment. Putting gloves on would be too bulky for the detailed work he needed to do. He accepted the fact that he would just have to work in pain.

Laughing, John said, "I can pretend I'm Michael Jackson at bedtime. Only I'll have to wear just one glove."

"I'm not sleeping with Michael Jackson," I bantered. "You can wear two."

"Let's talk about the lotion I need all over my body. Sounds kinky. But I will need help. There are some places I can't reach."

"Honey, I will be glad to help you with that."

It became a daily ritual. He left for work before me, so I was still home when he showered. When I heard the shower water turn off, I would go in the bathroom prepared to slather him with cream. When I bent to rub it on his legs, he would rest his hand on my head, sometimes apologizing for being so much trouble. After his original reluctance, he finally understood this was a gift of love and it became a special bonding time. We always ended with a kiss.

On July 19th, John received a text from a techie friend who knew the Mac he ordered had arrived.

"How's that new Mac?"

John: "I haven't opened it yet. Joy and I have gone out to dinner."

"What? You didn't take it to dinner with you?"

John: "Do you know my wife?"

CHAPTER FIVE

Seaside, Oregon was one of our getaway places. Life had been happening so fast, we felt the need to decompress. John loved the ocean…me not so much. But the boardwalk that paralleled the beach was far enough away from the roar for me to enjoy holding his hand while we walked and talked. No subject was off limits. It seemed we vacillated between light, delightful topics, with a heavy-duty one occasionally thrown in. It was during those strolls I became privy to his innermost thoughts. Our deep abiding faith in God allowed us to dissect our feelings without dread of the future.

We returned home in time for John's pre-op appointment with Dr. Fong on July 23rd. "I will be removing the lymph node on the left side of your neck. It's a mass in there, so I'm not sure what I'm getting in to. I may have to do a scope down your throat, or possibly remove your adenoids and tonsils. Before surgery, you need to watch this movie about tonsillectomies." The movie was rather lengthy and showed many details.

John was given four different consent papers to sign. This was far more complicated than I had thought. He was given a prescription for Lortab for the upcoming pain, with directions to always take it with food. Next on the agenda was an EKG and blood work. We were to arrive at Lourdes Hospital at 10:30 on the 26th and check in at the registration desk. John was to take no medication except his blood pressure pill.

Yet we still enjoyed life. He rode his bike whenever he had a chance. There was always a friend or two ready and willing to ride with him.

We went out to dinner with friends. And we continued to be in touch with the Starbucks Gang.

John figured out what to do with those cracks in his hands that were causing so much pain and difficulty. It all came about by accident. At the lab, working with models of teeth at various stages of creation, he used a very strong super glue. One day John noticed that an especially painful crack was no longer hurting. He had inadvertently glued it shut. His lightbulb came on. He mentioned his discovery at Starbucks and found out a friend had a painful cut. The next day he arrived at Starbucks with glue in his pocket. What a friend.

We arrived promptly at 10:30 on Thursday, the 26th to check in at Lourdes Hospital. By 11:30 John was moved to the pre-op room where the doctor and anesthesiologist spoke with him. At noon, he was taken to surgery and I was left to wait. He was brought back to the pre-op room at 1:30.

"I did not put you clear under. You were talking to me throughout the surgery. I had to go deeper than I thought, but I did not have to take out your tonsils. I did have to pull some muscle aside to get to the node. I will need you back here next Wednesday. You need to sleep propped up tonight and can remove the bandage tomorrow. Put Neosporin on the site and don't let water hit it."

Well, we're back to the recliner. It was nice while it lasted.

By 2:00 we had filled out the necessary paperwork for release and headed home. On the way, John received a phone call from his brother, Jim, who lived in Nevada. He was playing in a golf tournament in Spokane and had an evening off. Could he come for a brief visit? So, we went out to dinner, with John receiving curious stares. The bandage went all the way around his neck, and it looked like someone had tried to cut off his head. Jim followed us to our house and even though John was tired, they spent several hours talking before John fell asleep and his brother returned to Spokane.

John received a text from our daughter, Lorri.

"Thinking of you dad. Prayers for your recovery. Love you.

John: "Love U2."

Lorri: "Isn't that a rock band? Ha-ha."

On the first of August we returned to Dr. Fong's office for him to remove the stitches. "The preliminary report shows T-cell lymphoma – anaplastic. You need to see Dr. Ness tomorrow."

I tried to remember what it was like to live through a day without juggling pills and doctors. In the space of just a few short months we had begun living in a surreal world, but our peace remained. We took each day as it came.

Once again, we entered Dr. Ness's office. It was a comfort to know we had a very caring doctor. As he began to talk, his concern for John's well-being came through.

"I've received the pathology report and consulted with Dr. Shustov. Your lymphoma has no B-cells. That changes the treatment a little. He recommends a fifth drug that will be delivered over a three-day period and will take one to one and a half hours each day. It's not a very harsh drug but might compound the side effects. We will add it for the first round and see how you do. It's usually given to people under the age of sixty. Gloria will be the nurse navigator and counselor for your chemo. One drug, the side effect can affect the pumping of your heart, so we will have to check for fluid retention. You may have a problem with nausea, so some anti-nausea med will be put in the chemo IV. Do not take any aspirin. Your energy will be at the lowest at seven to fourteen days. In five to eight days, you may get sores in your mouth. After twenty-one days you will rebound and that's when we do another cycle. You will need a thermometer to take your temperature regularly. 100.4 is the cutoff. If it goes higher, you will be hospitalized. Here's the plan. You will be given CHOEP, chemo for peripheral non-Hodgkin's – large cell T-cell lymphoma. This is an aggressive form and only six percent of people have this kind."

He handed us information about the chemo. There were five pages of side effects and precautions for each of the five types of treatment to be given him. Cytoxan, Etoposide, Vincristine, Adriamycin and Prednisone would be infused one bag at a time. The Prednisone was to help the IV chemo drugs work better.

"You will go to the Infusion Center for three days and since each bag has to be done separately, you will be there most of the day. On the fourth day you will come back here for a Neulasta shot. This is given after chemo to stimulate growth of healthy white blood cells in the bone marrow."

Neulasta had only four pages of side effects and precautions, mentioning it might cause bone pain.

Here was the schedule we were handed.

8/13/12 – 10:00 am - chemo
8/14/12 – 8:30 am
8/15/12 – 8:00 am
8/16/12 – 9:00 am – shot
8/20/12 – 4:45 pm – Dr Ness
9/4/12 – 8:30 am – Dr. Ness
9/4/12 – 10:00 am – chemo
9/5/12 – 8:00 am
9/6/12 – 8:00 am
9/7/12 – 9:00 am – shot
Along with 19 pages of instructions.

Dr. Ness continued. "You have a more aggressive type so we will start with three cycles of chemo and then radiation on your neck. Several weeks after treatment we will do another PET scan. We are assuming the worst case, so we are starting with CHO-EP, which is designed for the aggressive type. You are in an early stage of systemic. Several things need to be done before we can start treatment. You need a heart scan to make sure your heart can handle the chemo. You need to have a port inserted for the chemo, so it won't damage your skin. A thought flicked through my mind. *It can damage his skin and we are putting it in his body? Is there something wrong with that picture?* We will begin with chemo three weeks apart and then radiation four weeks after the chemo. A word of warning, the Prednisone may cause difficulty sleeping and make you cranky. *Oh goodie.* Our plan to is start the chemo two weeks from now. We will monitor your blood very carefully. You may not be able to work for nine to twelve weeks. Six weeks after you complete the chemo, we will do another PET scan. Kadlec will call about the heart scan and the placement of the port."

I only thought I was on overload before. If I hadn't known God was right there with me, I would have succumbed to utter terror. I had done some research. CHOEP was just various types of poison. His future looked horrifying, which translated to my outlook too. But with our exit from the doctor's office, we handed all that ugliness to God and looked forward to a relaxing evening, which probably included a nap for him.

CHAPTER SIX

D r. Kincaid was a general surgeon and a new name to place in my binder. On August 8th, we were in his office to discuss the upcoming insertion of a medi-port. John was given the go-ahead for the placement in two days. But before that could happen, John needed to undergo a heart scan to make sure he could handle the chemo. The scan was scheduled for the next day and it took an hour and forty-five minutes. They injected a liquid into his blood and then hooked him to a machine to check his heart function. Pictures of what was happening were shown on a screen. Apparently, it was okay.

It's hard to believe that with all these appointments, we both continued to work.

On Friday, the 10th of August, once again we drove to Dr. Kincaid's office. Check-in was at 11:45. First John was asked a lot of questions like, "Did you walk here?" I thought that odd. We were introduced to the anesthesiologist, Elle, from Armenia. By 2:15, the surgery was over, and John came walking back into the waiting room complete with a medi-port. He was given a prescription for Percocet and told to come back on Monday to get the stitches out.

At home, I helped him change clothes into something comfortable. When he removed his shirt, I did a doubletake. John was a very hairy man, and now he was lopsided. His right chest had been shaved. "Go look in the mirror. You'll be surprised." We had a good laugh.

After he was settled in his big chair for a nap, I entered the kitchen. It was time to do something about all these doctors and medicines. I cleared out a cupboard, arranged the medicines by time of day to be taken, and attached an Excel spreadsheet on the door to keep track of what doctor was responsible for what. A blood pressure machine, blood glucose monitor and the various other accoutrements for his medical care occupied the counter below. The paraphernalia of a potentially terminal illness had usurped the space in our kitchen. I had become his home care provider.

That evening, nineteen people gathered in our home to celebrate completion of a training for prospective elders that had been held at the church for the past nine months. When we built our house in 2010, we felt God leading us to design it for outreach. At that time, I had never given a party and pretty much argued with God for a few months. He won. So, every four months since we moved in, we had given a party. Our first one had sixty people. This small party was just an extra in that party schedule.

Three days later, we walked into what was called Short Stay in the Trios Hospital building. Neither John nor I had any experience with chemo. We had no clue what an infusion center entailed. The room was rectangle shaped with recliner-type chairs along the walls. There were six chairs on one side and four on the other. On the side with fewer chairs, at the opposite end from the entry door, was the nurse's desk. John was escorted all the way to the chair across from that desk.

We would be here all day, so I had my crocheting and a book to read if he fell asleep. We got him covered up and comfortable. It was very quiet. Five other people were hooked up to those hanging bags of poison. John was the only one who had a companion. *That's so sad. Don't they have anyone who cares enough to sit with them?*

First, they started with a saline solution to clean out the medi-port. Then came the first bag of chemo. *How do I know what to look for? What could happen?* We talked softly, both unsure of what came next.

I heard harp music. As I looked around to see where it might be coming from, John asked, "Do you hear harp music?"

A little of my playful side crept out. "Do you hear harp music, John?"

"Yes. Where is it coming from?"

About that time, the door at the other end of the room opened and a lady entered, carrying what seemed to be a portable harp, playing as she walked.

John called to her from his chair, "You need to give us some warning. I thought I had passed over."

Laughter. That's how to lighten the atmosphere in an infusion center.

After all five bags had been administered, the nurse gave him two different prescription bottles for nausea. "Take one. If two hours later you are still nauseous, take the other one."

We headed home with more prescriptions to add to our supply. Within hours, John developed non-stop hiccups, one of the side effects. He experienced several cycles into the evening and on into the night. Makes sleeping difficult.

Day two we were back at Short Stay. Except for the hiccups, there had been no noticeable difference in John. So far, he hadn't needed the medicine for nausea.

August 15th, day three, we had to be there at 8:00 am. As the day transpired, I began to notice changes in John. His skin color no longer looked healthy. He wasn't needing to go to the bathroom. He lay motionless and slept. I mentioned my concerns, but it seemed this was all part of the program. When he was through, I took him home. As the evening passed, John began experiencing a new development; diarrhea.

The next day I took a very lethargic John to Dr. Ness's office to receive his Neulasta shot, which was administered by the nurse Laila. Side note: single dose – $7,089. "You can exercise, just don't push too hard. You need to save your energy." She dismissed my concerns. I was in uncharted territory for me and wasn't sure how hard to push. I took him home. But something still wasn't right. I just felt it. I stood by his bed and said, "John you need to get up. I want to take you back to the doctor."

"I'll be better tomorrow."

I waited awhile and returned to the bedroom. No improvement. I repeated my request. He repeated his answer.

The third time there was no improvement, I changed my words. "John, either you get up, put on your pants and let me help you to the car, or I'm calling an ambulance."

"Why are you talking to me like that?"

"It's my tough love voice. You are not okay."

He got up, put on his pants, I put him in the car and returned to Dr. Ness's office. We were taken to the office of the nurse navigator named Gloria. After I spoke with her, she left and came back with an appointment for John to see Dr. Ness the next day. "No, he needs to be seen now." After some stalling on her part, she said okay and placed us in an examining room.

Dr. Ness came in at 4:30. One look at John and he knew he wasn't okay. He started with weighing him. He had gained twelve pounds in three days. His blood sugar was off the chart. His kidney function had deteriorated. His scrotum was swollen.

"Do not take Furosemeide in the morning. I need to call Dr. Markle regarding your blood sugar. You need a diuretic IV tonight and another tomorrow morning. Then come see me. Start the prescription for heartburn and take the prescription for the hiccups. Tomorrow we will do some X-rays. "Then he sent him to Short Stay for the diuretic IV. When that was completed, they gave us a urinal for John to use in the car on the way home in case he couldn't make it. He didn't need it. His kidneys were still not working.

Next day, the 17th of August, John had a 9:00 am appointment with Dr. Kincaid to get his stitches out. But he was scheduled to get an X-ray first. As we waited, I spied a wheelchair at the end of the hall, and he sat in that in the waiting room. It was easier for him to sleep in the chair. We waited an hour, and I finally went to the counter to see why it was taking so long. They proceeded to search for his paperwork.

"We seem to have lost his paperwork. We even looked in the trash. We're just not really sure what happened. We are so sorry." He was immediately taken to X-ray where we were informed they were not at all backed up. He could have been seen immediately. Oh well.

At 11:00 John went to Short Stay for another diuretic IV. While I sat beside him, he received a phone call from the NW Cancer Clinic that he needed to come by and fill out the paperwork for his radiation that was scheduled to start on the 24th. I was so grateful for my binder so I could keep track.

John received a text from a friend:

"Just thinking about you. God be with you. Will we see you in the morning?"

John: "I should be there, pending some health issues." He shared his response with me. I didn't say much but thought a lot. *Really? Does he not even know how sick he is? He thinks he's meeting someone in the morning?*

When the IV was done, we traveled up in the elevator to Dr. Ness's office. The news was not good. His kidneys were still not functioning, he was dehydrated, and his blood sugar was way too high. Dr. Ness called for a wheelchair and told me John was being admitted to the hospital (which was in the same building) for a day or two. He needed some longer-term diuretic IV, which I did not understand since he was dehydrated. But I would ask about that later.

More tests. An EKG and Echocardiogram and then an ultrasound of his kidneys. Next was a chest X-ray. I was exhausted and I wasn't even the patient.

Two days later, a Saturday, Dr. Ness came by with his analysis of the situation. He was always so caring and gentle. Even though his words were like projectiles, his demeanor lessoned the blow.

"You have nephrotic syndrome. I've been in consultation with Dr. Tendon, (a partner of John's kidney doctor, Dr. Arif). He thinks the Prednisone triggered it. By the way, the X-rays showed you have had a previous heart attack. It must have been a silent one. Your heart function is normal. You're anemic. I've checked with Dr. Markle. You need to go on insulin. Call my office on Monday and make an appointment for Tuesday."

With a pat on John's leg, he told us we could go home.

Dr. Tendon dropped by with some last-minute instructions. "Start taking the Benicar again. Take the potassium for two days. Check your blood pressure for the next three to four days. And make an appointment to see Dr. Arif next week."

But before we could leave, we needed training in administering the insulin shot. Some nurses came in with a glucose monitor and insulin. We were then taught about the two different types of insulin he would be injecting. One was fast-acting and did not have to be refrigerated. The other one was long-term and did need the refrigerator. There was to be lots of checking his blood sugar. He was given a sliding scale to help figure out how many units he needed. We also needed to get a Sharps container to put his needles in. The syringes were for a one-time use. Next, he was shown how to give himself the shot. I was writing notes as fast as I could and hoping he was understanding what they were saying.

He was now insulin dependent.

I had no medical training. It was very daunting to take this man home who had so many things wrong. What was I supposed to look for? As John slept on the way home, I had a long talk with God.

Oh God, I sure need your guidance. I don't know how to do all this, and I'm not sure he does either. But our eyes are on you. Thank you so much for being with us.

CHAPTER SEVEN

The morning of August 20th, we walked to the garage, climbed in our car and headed out.

But for me, it wasn't that simple. "Where exactly are we going? I forget which doctor we are seeing this morning. Do you know? Otherwise, I need to pull over and confirm with my calendar." The doctor appointments were all just a jumble in my head. But John knew. "Yes, Joy, I am scheduled to see Dr. Arif." That did not totally answer my question. Since I was driving, I needed clarification. "Okay. Thanks. But I don't remember his location exactly."

John knew right where we were going, gave me directions and in a matter of minutes we pulled into Dr. Arif's parking lot. It all came flooding back. I was familiar with Dr. Arif since he had been John's nephrologist for several years. One of his congenial traits was that his nickname for John was Boss. There was no waiting. After some brief remarks, and taking John's vitals, Dr. Arif began talking.

"You are dehydrated because of the side effect of Prednisone. We will not give that to you again. Be sure and take your Furosemeide and Aldactone once a day. I will give you a prescription for potassium. You already have a prescription from Dr. Ness, so finish his first and then begin with mine. Do not ever use any salt. I believe you will never go off insulin now. I am working closely with Dr. Ness, and we are going to get you better, Boss."

John needed blood work done before he saw Dr. Ness the next morning. He had shivered all night and I was relieved we were headed to see the doctor. When we got there, he was shaking so forcefully he was unable to walk. I entered the front door of the doctor's building and retrieved a wheelchair from the foyer. Once seated, his intense body movement began propelling the wheelchair. I placed him against the wall and ran to my car. I knew I had a blanket in my trunk, so left him sitting there to retrieve it. Soon he was snuggled under Dale Earnhardt (I was the NASCAR fan). But he was too sick to notice or care.

Blood work completed, we traveled up in the elevator. I pushed the wheelchair to the counter in Dr. Ness's office and asked for a room. "John needs to lay down." We transferred him to an examining table and covered him with my blanket. He was still shaking excessively. Since I was familiar with Short Stay, I knew they had heated blankets. I traveled down the elevator and returned with two of them. John slept until Dr. Ness entered. One look at the doctor's face and I knew John was in trouble.

"John has zero white blood cells. The cutoff for hospitalization is a temp of 100.4. Let's take his temp." The thermometer registered 100.6. While we waited for paperwork, Dr. Ness called Dr. Markle and briefly explained the situation. John's platelets were just too low. They discussed a preventive antibiotic and Imodium for his diarrhea.

A wheelchair arrived for John, and he was pushed from the room. Dr. Ness handed me the papers and said I would have to go down to admitting. As I walked, I read them. I saw words like "guarded condition" and "renal failure". He was admitted to the Critical Care Unit. I hurried home to get our stuff. When I came back, there was a sign on his door saying to wear a mask, wash hands, no fruit or flowers, etc. The recliner chair beside his bed became my home.

Through the night his temp stayed above 100. We were kept busy all night helping him to the bathroom with episodes of diarrhea. Next morning, I asked the nurse if they were giving him Imodium like they had told me they would. She checked. They weren't. The reason. Because he needed to keep his bowels moving to rid his body of the chemo. *Is this supposed to be making any sense?*

As John lay on the starched white sheets, feverish and fatigued, a nurse checked his vitals. She spoke to him about his touch and go condition. He roused from his lethargy and said very clearly, "Either way, it's okay."

The nurse quickly glanced at me. "Does he know what he said?"

"Yes. We are very aware of his condition. But we have absolute peace that this is in God's hands. We are not worried about the outcome."

Many times over the next days, weeks, months and years we were able to repeat those wonderful words to others.

The next day was our daughter Lorri's birthday. I thought I had contacted her but wasn't sure. At noon, some friends came by. Glenda brought me lunch and Larry sat with John while I visited with Glenda in another room. They offered to stay, allowing me to go home, shower and change clothes.

Night and day had blended together. John remained tethered to an IV stand, with more than one fluid dripping into his body. Orange sherbet became the meal of the day, since it was all he could tolerate. A man dressed as a doctor came into the room and stood by John's bed. I didn't know who he was and had to ask. "My name is Dr. McKune. Dr. Ness is on vacation, but he asked me to come by and check on John. I'm to report back to him tonight." He turned to John, "Your white cells still have not recovered. Your electrolytes are out of whack. We will give you Gatorade or something with electrolytes in it."

Finally, that evening John's temp dropped below 100. Through the night it continued downward and at 7:00 am it was 98.6. His white blood cell count was .05. Improvement.

At noon, my food angel brought me lasagna, salad and a roll from Casa Mia. Once again Larry stayed with John while I devoured the wonderful food in another room with Glenda. My mouth stayed full, so she had to do the talking.

Toward evening, Dr. Ness came by. "We are backing off on the antibiotic since it is hard on the kidneys and causing diarrhea. Your white blood cell count is now 200. It needs to be 2,000 so you will be here a day or two more. But you are trending up."

Trying to tempt John with something to eat, at noon the next day I drove to Yoke's and brought him a baked potato. Since it is one of my favorite foods, I had one too. While we were eating, Dr. Ness came by.

"I've canceled the mask protocol. Your white blood cells are slowly rebuilding. Your kidney function was greatly affected by the antibiotic. You need to eat protein. And see if you can walk the loop in the hallway."

When he left, we walked it twice.

At 7:00 am the next morning, John was freed from the IV, which made it much easier to walk the hall. Then the parade of doctors began. Dr. McKune was first and gave us his cell phone number if we needed him over the weekend. Next was Dr. Arif. He gave John instructions on which prescriptions to take and which ones to stop, to get his blood work done on Monday and send the results to him. Then Dr. McKune returned.

"You can do activity as tolerated. Your creatine is coming down. Take the Zofran as needed at home."

John asked about the Hanford tour we had signed up for. He had really wanted to do that, so I had stayed up past midnight the night the tickets went on sale. I knew they would sell out fast. Because of his compromised immunity, he was told to cancel. Then more instructions about various prescriptions. By 9:40 a new team was in our room to give John two pills and then put some Nexium through the port to prevent ulcers from the chemo. More nurses with more details about insulin.

"You need to keep a chart. Take a shot before each meal and one at bedtime. Watch the number and make sure it doesn't go too low. But you need to make an appointment with Dr. Markle to get your final instructions."

My head was spinning.

Through all of this, John never lost touch with his dentists. They were more than a name to him. He knew their families, births and deaths. They had no idea what he was dealing with.

He received a text from Lorri:

"Hearing your voice was the best birthday present this year! Glad you feel better. Love you, Dad."

Apparently, we hadn't forgotten it.

After five days in the hospital, John was discharged.

CHAPTER EIGHT

There was no time for a break. All too soon we started the rounds of doctors. First was Dr. Ness.

"Your weight is stable. You are still anemic. I'm thinking you need a blood transfusion before the next chemo. I've consulted with Dr. Shustov and we are cutting your next treatment down to 80% of what we gave you before. The Prednisone will be cut by 50%. I have been in touch with Dr. Arif regarding your kidneys. He will be in charge of your phosphorous/magnesium dose. You need to see Dr. Markle in two weeks for an insulin schedule. Remember to get your blood work done on the 4th at 7:30 before you see me at 8:00. Two to three months after your radiation, we will need to do another PET scan. John, I was really worried about you while I was on vacation. I hated to leave. But I checked in with Dr. McKune and we talked exhaustively. It's so good to see you better."

After a discussion about a blood transfusion, which John declined, we left Dr. Ness's office feeling encouraged. Even though he had some appetite, John said all food tasted like cardboard. I didn't ask when he had ever eaten that. I scoured the grocery store searching for something to tempt him. I remembered that in one of the discussions about chemo, we were told sometimes it made people crave something pickled. I bought cans of pickled beets. You would have thought I had made him a German chocolate cake. He ate a whole can.

The next day we made a brief visit to Dr. Arif. He gave some instructions about two new prescriptions we were to pick up. Then we drove to Dr. Markle's, where we received precise instructions about

John checking his blood sugar, when he would need to take insulin and how many units.

"Next week, drop your meter off so we can download the information on it. That will help us know how we are doing. Increase your Lantus to twelve units and keep increasing it by two units until the morning reading is less than 150. If it's greater than 140, add two more units. If it gets too low, less than 80 or 90, you will get dizzy and shaky."

We had a few days respite before the next round of chemo. We held hands as we walked and talked. We sat at the dining room table and prayed. It was difficult to think of going back for more of that stuff that almost killed him. But our peace remained.

By 10:00 am on the 4th of September, John was once again hooked up to the IV. His blood work that morning had shown his white blood cell count was a little high, which they said was good, explaining that was the result of the Neulasta injection. His blood sugar was too high at 308. But the bags continued to be emptied until he had gone through all five.

On the third day, when they removed the IV from his port, the blood began to spurt. John had to hold his finger on it until they could apply pressure and get it stopped. It seemed there was always something new to deal with. When we got home and he took his blood sugar, it was 440, so he gave himself ten units. I remained very alert to any changes in his behavior.

One more Neulasta shot, and we were through with this round. By Saturday, the nausea began. He was now taking sixteen pills a day. That alone would make me nauseous.

From Lorri:

"Thinking of you, Dad. Hope you are getting some good naps with your buddy Charlie. Love you."

John: "Thanks. I am feeling stronger today, a little bit at a time. Charlie is taking good care of me, as is Mom."

Lorri: "Wish I was there."

The 10th saw us back in Dr. Arif's office. Again, I took notes as fast as I could. Stop this and take that. Do this and don't do that. But his kind heart was evident as he gave his instructions to Boss.

"You have acute renal failure and are in Stage 3 kidney disease. I've spoken with Dr. Ness. He is prescribing FloMax for at least a month for your prostate. Your blood count is still recovering nicely. Boss, come back in three weeks and be sure to have blood work done first."

It seemed the merry-go-round of doctors would never end. Dr. Markle was the next day.

"You can go as high as 30-40 units on the Lantus. You want to keep your reading between 150-200. Stop drinking any liquid after 5:00 pm. We'll wait and see if we think you need more antibiotic. Your white blood count is okay. You are anemic, but we will hold off on a blood transfusion for now. You will need a PET scan to check and see if the nodes are gone. A CT scan with contrast is harmful to the kidneys. They are doing great, so we don't want to compromise them."

John asked, "I have a business meeting in San Antonio next month that's been planned for a long time. Any chance I can still go?"

He received approval.

Three days later we were in the office of Dr. Sheila Rege for evaluation and counseling. She would be responsible for John's radiation. She had received the PET scan and pointed out on the picture that John had calcified gallstones. Who knew?

"We will do a low dose of radiation. For T-cell it's only 3,000 to 3,600. The mumps gland has a problem with radiation so there may be some complications there. We will give it Monday through Friday – five days a week – for four weeks. Each treatment will be twenty minutes long. Side effects will be limited to that area. You will look like you've had too much sun exposure, and you will no longer be able to grow a beard on that side. It may affect your tongue, and it can affect your teeth. Go see a dentist before we start and get any needed dental work done. Radiation cannot be performed until you have completed your chemo, so come back on the 11th or 12th. That will be our planning session. Then on the 15th or 16th we will do a simulation. We plan to start radiation on October 22nd."

The proposed radiation schedule:

10/22 – 10/25
10/29 – 11/2
11/5 – 11/9
11/12 – 11/16

We had many questions after that little speech.

"What's a simulation?"

"There are three steps to get ready.

Take a picture of inside

Plan on that picture

Merge with the real person – a planning X-ray

If they merge, we will go ahead."

That didn't help me a whole lot.

I asked, "We have a weekend trip planned to Phoenix and will be returning on November 12th. Is he allowed to miss any radiations?"

I didn't mention it was to attend a NASCAR race. We had priorities. Months before we had made plans to travel to the second home of one of our Starbucks friends. We would stay with them and several of us would attend the race. A reprieve was granted.

"He may miss only one. You need to take into account that he will be tired, but probably not as bad as he was after chemo. His whole body will be working on healing and will be using his energy for that."

John was claustrophobic. When the scans had been done, he had been on a table inside a very noisy tube and had to lay perfectly still. But he was not restrained and could have climbed out if he panicked. I had asked him how he handled it.

"I went inside my head and very far away."

So the next explanation was truly overwhelming for him.

"You will be fitted with a mesh mask which will be molded to your face and shoulders. It will be screwed to the table so you cannot move for the duration of the radiation."

That evening we were a little somber. The impending loss of freedom enclosed in a machine weighed heavily on him. By bedtime, we had given it to God and could once again rest in peace.

9/14/12 – text from a friend

"Are you okay? Can we help you or Joy? We are praying for both of you."

John: "I'm feeling weak but okay."

9/18/12 – text to Tammi and Jim

"Got a real nice lighthouse card from you today. Thanks for both the card and the prayers. I'm doing pretty good, just weak sometimes."

Tammi: "Glad you like the card. Hang in there."

CHAPTER NINE

O n the 20th of September, John developed a bad cold and very loose cough, and pneumonia was a concern. I had a long talk with God. *"God, we believe you are in control of every part of this journey. I'm asking you to touch John and keep pneumonia from developing. We have felt your presence through all the various health episodes he's experienced so far. We give our concern about pneumonia to you. We are so grateful for the peace that reigns in our hearts."* His love surrounded us night and day and it was such a blessing and relief to be held in His arms.

Early the next morning I called to ask if Dr. Ness could see him. No answer, so I left a message. Laila returned the call at 5:30 that evening. "It's too late for the doctor to see him now. Just take him to an urgent care clinic." We didn't want to, so we just waited for his next appointment in three days.

Dr. Ness checked John out. Even though his cough indicated a problem, his lungs sounded good, and he had no fever. The doctor rolled his stool to face John, placed his hand on John's knee and began to talk. "We'll go ahead with the third round of chemo. A PET scan had been scheduled, but it was canceled due to a conflict with Group Health. They don't allow PET scans at Kadlec Hospital, so it has been re-scheduled to be done at Trios Hospital in two weeks. Come back and see me in ten days."

As we left his office my mind was unsettled. *Just how sick do they have to be to cancel the procedure? Apparently, John isn't sick enough. God, give Dr. Ness the wisdom and guidance he needs to make this decision.*

The third round of chemo came and went. We were old hands at this now. We were on a first-name basis with the nurses. It seemed strange to be so at home in that place we had viewed with such trepidation only a few weeks before.

And then John was through with chemo.

We discovered chemo affects many areas of the body. As John rested, his lower jaw began to swell. Within hours he was in severe pounding pain with an abscessed tooth. He took Tylenol, but it didn't even begin to help. When the pharmacy opened the next morning, I was there with written instructions that had been given to John for pain from two different doctors, prescriptions which we had never filled.

"Which one of these is the strongest? That's the one I need to get."

The pharmacist chose Percocet. I took it home and John began a regimen that day and into the night. Soon he was throwing up and seemed delirious. It was a bad night.

The next day was Sunday, but John had a good relationship with his dentist clientele. He called one, Dr. Boudro. After explaining his issue, the doctor called in a prescription for Penicillin and told John to take Zofran to stop the vomiting. I made one more trip to the pharmacy, brought home the prescription, and gave the pill to John. In only a matter of minutes he had thrown it up.

Monday morning, we stopped to get John's blood work done for Dr. Arif's appointment and from there I took him to Dr. Boudro's office. After an examination and then consultation with Dr. Ness, Dr. Boudro extracted the culprit. John was given a different prescription for the pain, Vicodin. After taking the pain pill, he slept all day, not eating or drinking. Since he seemed incapacitated by the medicine, I canceled Dr. Arif's 4:40 appointment. But I did ask about the results of the blood work. "His kidney function is improved, and the white blood count is good. Let's just get him through this dental complication."

Wednesday we were back in Dr. Ness's office. Always so friendly and caring, he just warmed my heart. I knew he was doing his best. After the preliminaries, John told him, "I have this funny feeling in my mouth."

"It's just part of the reaction to chemo. It takes up to three weeks to get the chemo out of your system, but the side effects last several months. Your PET scan is scheduled for next week on the 15th. It will tell us how well we've done in getting rid of your cancer."

During all the physical difficulties, John arrived at the conclusion two motorcycles was more than he could handle. He had now dropped the larger and heavier RT three times, breaking the side mirror each time. The word that his BMW R1150 RT was for sale spread like wildfire through the riding community. Within days, it no longer resided in our garage.

Text from a friend:

"How are you feeling? Are you glad it's over? How much rest before the radiation? I can't wait to see you and talk about how you are doing."

John: "Feeling tired and weak, but okay. I had to have a tooth extracted on Monday morning. That kind of set me back, but I'll tell you all about it tomorrow."

On the 9th we drove to Trios for the re-scheduled PET scan. The technician, Rodney, was very friendly and let me stay in the room until the Xanax took affect. John had explained his claustrophobia to Dr. Ness, so something had been prescribed to help alleviate his anxiety. *Perhaps it will help while he's in that machine.* I filled out papers and requested a copy of the two previous PET scans for Dr. Ness. I was told they would mail me a disk.

Two days later we were in the office of Dr. Rege.

"I've seen the results of the PET scan. Would you like to know what they are?"

Even though I felt it was Dr. Ness's place to tell us, we wanted to know now.

"The PET scan was clear. There are no more spots."

She continued to talk, but my mind was back at the word "clear". The chemo had worked. My heart was flooded with praises to God for His wonderful care for John. All I really heard from the doctor was that his first radiation was scheduled for the 22nd. We planned to arrive back in the TriCities at noon that day, coming home from our business meeting in San Antonio. An appointment was set for 5:15 that evening.

Somewhere in her talking she told John, "You will have a dry mouth because the radiation will hit a saliva gland, and your throat will be sore. Also, you will never be able to grow a good beard on that side and you may have a permanent goose neck. Swallowing may become difficult. You may have a problem with opening your mouth very wide, which can cause issues at the dentist. You will lose your sense of taste."

I had no idea what a goose neck was and didn't ask. We let all that information roll over us and focused on the word "clear". Our prayer had been that this cancer journey would not be wasted, that good would come of it. Even up to the day the PET scan showed the cancer was gone, we had shared many times about our peace when others would comment on our lack of stress. We truly believed that either way it was okay. But this report was awesome.

John sent a text to Lorri: "Just wanted to let you know we got the results of the PET scan today. It's all clear – negative – all gone. Great news! Praise the Lord!"

Lorri: "Praises!"

A few days later John had a checkup with Dr. Ness. "Your white cell count is still a little high and you are slightly anemic. Your kidneys and liver are okay. Dr. Markle needs to take over the insulin prescriptions. And I'll see you again in six weeks, on the 26th of November. Your next PET scan will be in January or February."

Maybe life will return to a semblance of normal.

There is actually a phenomenon known as chemo brain. It clouds the thinking and causes people to say and do strange things. As we reveled in the knowledge that his cancer was gone, we began talking about a party to celebrate our bonus round. Unbeknownst to me, John decided we needed more lawn chairs for our guests. He ordered four online from ShopKo.

John was out of town on a bike ride when four large boxes were delivered to our driveway. I asked a neighbor if he would help me get those boxes into the garage. As I investigated, I discovered John had ordered four boxes of lawn chairs, two to a box, that needed assembly. I briefly envisioned the chairs if John tried to put them together in his muddled state of mind. Since we had a care group that met at our house every Thursday evening, I called each one and turned the next Thursday meeting into a social; dinner and assembling chairs. It was hilarious to watch the engineer and medical doctor trying to work together over their chair. By the end of the evening, we had eight new lawn chairs in our back yard.

CHAPTER TEN

O ur next visit with Dr. Rege was on the 16th of October, a final check on John before beginning treatment. "Your first radiation is scheduled for the 22nd at 5:15. The rest of your appointments will probably be around 3:00. Since you are just across the parking lot, we will call when the previous patient leaves and you can walk over. On the 9th of November we will do it as soon as possible so you can leave town. You will lose the ability to taste, but that will be temporary. Use 100% aloe vera cream for your neck. Over time, your skin will change color and get much darker. Today we need to make your mask."

First, they had to make him comfortable on the radiation table, since he had a problem with his back. He liked to say the word, spon-dylolisthesis, which was his disorder. A vertebra in his lower back had slipped out of place, causing pain. Positioning a pillow under his knees helped. Next, they situated a wedge under his neck, so his chin was lifted and his head tipped back.

I watched as they took a sheet of plastic mesh, placed it in hot water, then lay it over his face and began to mold it to him. They used their hands to fit every inch of that plastic against his head, face, neck and shoulders. They even pulled it up to a point over his nose so he could breathe. Once it was tight against him, they used big plastic screws to fasten it to the table. This man who was claustrophobic was now immobilized. This was the simulation they had warned us about. Once the beam was shining in exactly the correct spot, they marked the plastic and then released him.

My heart went out to him. He knew he would be like that for twen-ty minutes during the actual radiation. On the way home, he shared about the experience. "I couldn't even swallow. What happens if I get choked? I'm going to need a lot of prayers for this procedure." The requests we lifted to God became very detailed about John's need for calm while in the machine.

On Halloween, John and our dog Charlie had a delightful evening. We had about one hundred little, and some not so little, trick or treaters. One stands out, a little girl who got her candy and then turned to yell at her parents standing on the sidewalk. "They're old." John yelled, "Hey, we're not old. We're just dressed up that way."

Before we began the next installment of his health journey, we traveled to San Antonio. Once a year we met with very good friends in various places around the country, a few times in Mexico and once in Europe. We all belonged to a business organization started by John and a friend in 1989. We never missed a meeting and had been looking forward to this one for months. We knew we would receive lots of love and support as we gathered. Sometimes my daughter Tammi and her husband Jim who lived in California joined us for the fun, but this meeting was just too far to drive.

John sent a text to Lorri:

"We're here at the Riverwalk in San Antonio. Why don't you drive over and say hi? Thanks for all your good wishes. I feel great and am doing well."

Lorri: "Enjoy your time in San Antonio. Wish I could meet you there. Love you."

John: "Well, thank you. Love you back."

About halfway through the radiation treatments, we made that quick weekend trip to Phoenix we had asked Dr. Rege about. Several couples from our hometown went too. Three of the couples owned homes down there, so we all had a place to stay. John was not the NASCAR fan, so he went with some of our friends to other activities. I hung out with the die hards, sitting on the bleachers, shivering in my t-shirt in the 55-degree weather. They let me sit between them to help break the wind.

John received his last radiation procedure the Friday before Thanksgiving. What a time for rejoicing! Some very special people joined us at the Cancer Clinic for the ringing of the bell, signifying the completion of treatment. Even other patients and their families in the waiting room joined in the clapping. Years before our daughter, Lorri, had housed a foreign exchange student, Saskia, whom we had welcomed as part of our family. She and her fiancé Thomas came from Germany, along with Lorri from Georgia, to celebrate with us.

Later that evening, we opened our home to twenty-nine dear friends who joined us in giving thanks. John was determined cancer would not be the focus of our lives, so we continued our pattern of a party every four months. This get together was a combination of our annual dessert social and a time of expressing our gratitude.

On Thanksgiving, as we gathered around the table, my heart overflowed with blessings. especially one huge one. With God's help, John had been able to endure nineteen times fastened down and immovable inside that machine. Tammi and Jim had now joined us, and I drank it all in as each one took a turn in sharing what they were thankful for. There were no dry eyes.

But congratulations were also in order. One day sitting in Bob's Burgers eating lunch, Saskia announced with a big grin, "We will be three." It took John and me a moment. Then she pointed to her stomach. Ah. They were expecting a baby.

All too soon it was time for the goodbyes. More crying and hugs.

All the years I had known John, he had never been able to smell anything. One day, as we walked around in Costco, he asked, "What's that I smell?"

"You smell something?"

And then it hit him. He could smell. That happened about the same time he lost all sense of taste. You win some, you lose some. Radiation causes strange reactions.

The last week of November, John had an appointment with Dr. Ness. "Your blood counts are fine. Your liver is fine. You can stop taking the potassium but continue with the Mag Oxide. Your kidney function is worse but let Dr. Arif address that. Still refrain from taking any aspirin. Do you want the port out? If you require more chemo, they will have to put it back in."

"Yes, please remove it."

"Dr. Kincaid will make an appointment with you for that. Your next PET scan is in February. I will want to see you after that."

Before John was diagnosed with cancer, Lorri had offered us a timeshare for July 2013, in Banff, Canada. We had always wanted to go there. During his odyssey, it had sometimes looked doubtful we would make it. But now the trip was back in our conversations.

To John from Lorri:

"I hope you and mom have a wonderful time in Banff. I am so grateful you have that time to look forward to. Time has become so much more precious. Love you, Dad."

John: "Thank you so much for the opportunity to go. Yes, I am playing in the bonus round. ☺"

Lorri: "Will you ride your motorcycle? It should be gorgeous weather. I am happy to help you scratch something off your bucket list. I'll take good care of Charlie. Love you, Dad."

I was awakened early one morning with John singing, "Happy birthday to you." Not known for his exceptional vocal ability, I lay in the darkness grinning. How very special it was.

Our next doctor appointment was with Dr. Kincaid on the 10th of December for the removal of the port. I watched the procedure and requested to keep the port. With several stitches and a waterproof bandage, the doctor's instructions were, "Keep the dressing on for forty-eight hours. There is no need for any medicine to be applied. Come back in one week to have the stitches taken out."

Life had been traveling at breakneck speed. We chose Christmas to slow it all down, taking the week between Christmas and New Years to spend time with just us. The movie Les Miz was playing, but it was a bit tricky getting to the theater. The roads were extremely slick. We laughed at the misspelled word on the warning sign. "Drive slowly – snot and ice." That just about says it all. To finish off a Les Miz day, we came home and watched the 25th anniversary DVD.

I put away the Christmas decorations so lovingly placed the day after Thanksgiving by Saskia and Thomas. My beautiful memories bucket was full and running over. As I looked back over 2012, I marveled at the journey we had experienced. At the beginning of the year, we were totally unaware of what lay ahead. We had undergone a massive learning curve, but our confidence in God was now greater than it had ever been.

CHAPTER ELEVEN

The first day of January 2013, found us in a saloon for breakfast to celebrate New Year's with John's biker gang, a rather exclusive club of mostly BMWs. They had become very dear friends, even though those with Harleys made fun of those with BMWs. Harleys were very loud when started. Not so the BMWs. The Harley riders would yell out, "Can't hear it. Are you sure it started?"

For the first time in many years, we did not travel to Tempe, Arizona for an annual dental meeting the first week in January. It was always such fun to leave the cold and snow and walk around in t-shirts and eat Cold Slab ice cream. Sometimes I attended the seminars but sat in the back with my crocheting. One year, as I pulled the yarn high in the air to give me some slack to work with, the leader said, "Yes, Joy, did you have a question?" That elicited a laugh. Those who knew me, knew I really didn't care about how to make teeth. I was there to support my husband.

And Tempe was where I suffered one of my greatest embarrassments.

As a NASCAR fan for years, I was familiar with the sponsor logos on the side of the cars, including a Hooters emblem, an owl. The first time we had attended this conference in Tempe, after a day of meetings, we walked out the front door to find a place to eat. I could not contain my excitement.

"Look. There's a Hooters right across the street. Can we eat there?"

I'm sure my friends knew I was unaware what the slang word hooter meant. They all immediately agreed that would be the place to go. Ten of us crossed the street and climbed the stairs to the deck. When I saw the woman ushering us to a table, I did wonder about her lack of clothing. But it was when the waitress came to take my order, bent over close to my face and I was very aware of what I was looking at, that I understood. My face turned beet red, and my so-called friends erupted in raucous cheers and laughter. I wanted the floor to swallow me, and they never let me live that down. Every year, when discussing where to eat, they would always say, "We know Joy wants to eat at Hooters."

Therefore, when we decided we couldn't travel to Tempe this year, my delightful husband said, "I know you really want to eat at Hooters. I think the closest one is in Seattle. Do we need to drive over there?"

I gave him a knuckle punch.

We received a text from Paul Null

"I heard a rumor that the Bach Bed and Beverage might have space for an itinerant wedding parson and woman on the 31st and 1st."

John: "No rumor. It's a fact. We are really looking forward to your visit."

Me: "Yes, we are. The room is ready. Well, the mints aren't on the pillow yet."

Paul: "Yay!"

On the 31st a text came from Paul Null

"Be at your place by 6:30. Nulls would like to take Bachs to dinner at Renee's favorite Mexican place in Pasco. Okay?"

John: "That would be great. We would love to spend time with you guys. We might, however, have a little scramble about the check."

Paul: "Don't even think about bringing your wallet."

John: "Hey, I am no longer a chemo-addled wimp. I'm big and fat and I can take you out."

Paul: "LOL."

On the 15th of February, John heard from a friend

"I have a cold and won't be there in the morning. Don't want to spread it."

John: "I thought that's what friends are for."

All too soon, another issue arose. John began having a problem with his knee. He called Dr. Merrell, an orthopedic surgeon, for an appointment and got right in. After a time of consultation, Dr. Merrell said, "Not sure what's going on, but we will have to wait until after your PET scan before we can give you a cortisone shot."

Two days later John underwent another PET scan. A week later we were in Dr. Ness's office to get the results.

"You are cancer free. Stop taking the iron. The bad knee is probably related to the kidney. You have a spot on your kidney. Most likely it's just a cyst. Let's schedule an ultrasound to check it out. You'll have another PET scan in three months and then after that they will be scheduled for every six months."

In March it was time for our house anniversary party, celebrating three years in our new home. But this year was even more special. Forty-seven friends helped us rejoice in John's cancer free declaration. We called it our Bonus Round Party. After a wonderful evening of fun and laughter, we gathered in front of the fireplace.

John spoke:

"As most of you know, I went through a bout with cancer last summer. As Christ followers, Joy and I gave my treatment and outcome to God. Although I sure wanted to live, it was going to be up to Him. Gratefully, two different PET scan reports have shown that I am cancer free.

I remember talking to a friend after my treatment and he said he was proud of me for battling the cancer. I thought to myself, *it was never my battle*. I want to say thank you to those of you here that prayed for me and expressed the many well wishes I received during treatment. Thanks for an extraordinary kindness is extended to a neighbor who mowed my lawn most of the summer when I was too weak. And then there was a special trip Joy and I took to Phoenix with friends.

For a few years now we have wanted to get some new wedding rings, but never really looked hard for them. I guess it just wasn't a high priority. But now here I am…here we are…living the BONUS ROUND! So, to celebrate living without cancer, we purchased some rings and would like for you to be our witnesses as we say a few words to each other.

Joy, when I slipped that first wedding ring on your finger, I was totally clueless what marriage to you would be like. (We all laughed at that, including me.) Now these many years later, having experienced life with you, I want to put this new ring on your finger to indicate that, getting to know who you really are, I choose to spend my bonus round with you."

I spoke:

"A few months ago, I lived in the chair by your hospital bed as you lay there in guarded condition. We did not know the outcome of that journey, but we did know who was in control, and we were okay. And now you are cancer free.

So, we begin what we are calling our bonus round. Today, in front of our friends, we are placing new wedding rings on our fingers to symbolize our new journey together. As we face the future, I look forward to many great adventures with you, my best friend. My love for you is deeper than its's ever been."

CHAPTER TWELVE

L ife was looking up. Chemo and radiation were behind us, and John's strength was returning. But one day, walking out of Starbucks, he somehow twisted his leg as he took a step and heard a pop in his knee. Instant pain. Luckily, we already owned a cane.

Back we went to Dr. Merrell. "I'll give you a cortisone shot that will help you for two to three years. Wait a day or two after it's better before you go back to the gym. Let's do an MRI just to see what's going on." The shot and pain medicine helped a great deal. Once again, he could walk with no cane.

In a matter of days, we drove to KGH for John to undergo an ultrasound for the cyst in his kidney. The technician talked as he moved his probe. "Your bladder is still half full even though I just had you go to the bathroom. The kidney is failing to empty." He sent John to the bathroom and then checked again. "The kidney is not functioning as it should. And you have a lot of gallstones the size of peas."

It seemed John's body was a walking scientific laboratory. And on top of everything else, he was now experiencing dizzy spells.

Five days later, we were back in Dr. Merrell's office to hear the results of the MRI. "You have two tears in your meniscus, and I recommend outpatient surgery. You would be on crutches for a week, but it would take four to five weeks before you were back to full strength. The MRI shows results of old age wear and some calcium deposits. I'll give you a prescription for pain." Surgery was scheduled for March 28th, with a follow-up on April 9th.

The next day we were in Dr. Ness's office to find out the results of the ultrasound. "The cyst is not very large and shows no obstruction.

You do have an enlarged prostate, but none of this is cancer related. We'll do more blood work in three months and another PET scan in June. Not sure why you are experiencing dizziness. I suggest you see Dr. Markle for that."

Yet we continued to live, laugh and love. We took a weekend trip to visit John's daughter and family. She was graduating from rehab and invited us to the "coin out" celebration.

March 28th, surgery was completed about 10:30 in the morning. John was discharged with three new prescriptions to take on top of the eleven he was already ingesting. Dr. Merrell suggested he remember an acronym, PIER.

> P – Pain – keep it under control
> I – Ice – this is important
> E – Elevate – above the level of the heart
> R – Range of motion – do your exercises

Since we already owned some crutches, all we had to do was get them out of their resting place in the closet.

April began with a visit to Dr. Arif. It was short and not so sweet. Dr. Arif gently told John, "Boss, your kidney function is down to 35%. The protein level should be less than 1 and it is over 3. Your potassium is too high and you are in Stage 3 kidney failure. I want to check on you again in two months."

Next was a check-up by Dr. Merrell. "You are doing great. No hot tub for three weeks. It takes four to six weeks after surgery to be back to normal. If you haven't made progress in two to three weeks, I will send you to physical therapy. Otherwise, you don't have to come back."

And in my thoughts, *April…the month this all started one year ago.* My binder was full and so I began a new one. These weren't little binders; I had filled a 3" one. Not knowing what lay ahead, I started a new 3" one with the label **John's Continuing Journey**. Who knew so many doctors would be necessary in one year?

A scripture kept coming to me, so I looked it up in a King James version. "Let not your heart be troubled, neither let it be afraid." John 14:27 We were still trusting in Him. I had no idea how soon I would be leaning heavily on that verse.

A few weeks previously, I had kissed my husband goodbye and sent him off to work. At our dental lab, his job that day was to train a young lady from our local vo-tech school about how crowns were scanned, tweaked, and completed on our new machine. As he sat in front of the screen with her seated by his side, his mind went blank. After a brief pause, his thoughts connected again, and he continued his explanation.

Later she would tell me in that moment, his hands twitched. She thought he was having a seizure. But he made no mention of it to me. A few days later, at work, sitting in front of his computer composing an email to a dentist, again his mind went blank.

He thought, *that's weird.*

Little did I know he was keeping this secret from me.

Sitting in his cozy chair at home one evening watching television, he uttered an unusual sound. I looked up from my crocheting.

"What was that about?"

"Oh, nothing. I just felt odd for a minute."

Okay, what does it mean to feel odd? Is this something we need to explore? He could give me no better explanation.

That weekend was a motorcycle rally in another state, one he attended every year. John had endured chemo and radiation and didn't feel he was up to full strength. So, he asked two friends to ride with him as he traveled...on the motorcycle. They made it safely. He rode and rested as the weekend transpired, and then the friends escorted him home.

Monday morning, he was delivering dental cases. One dentist just happened to be close to the hospital. He thought *if I can find a parking space close to the entrance, I might go in and have them check me out. I still feel a little strange.*

That is so not like my macho husband. I would say he must have been feeling especially peculiar to choose to enter the ER.

A parking spot was available right by the emergency room door. John walked in and said, "My heart is feeling a little funny...." That's all he got out before someone yelled "wheelchair" and he was taken right back to an exam room. He called me from that room.

"I'm about to make your day go bad. I'm in the emergency room at Kadlec. I'm just not feeling right."

Of course, I was in a hurry to get to him. I had never driven to Kadlec Hospital in Richland from where I worked in Pasco. I had no idea the speed limit on the side street I drove down as a short cut to the freeway. Soon I had flashing lights in my rearview mirror. *Not now*, I thought. But yes, it was now. We went through the normal routine of license and registration. I asked, "Could we do this a little quicker? My husband has just been taken to the hospital." The very caring officer said, "Sure", and rapidly wrote the ticket. No empathy for what I had just explained.

When I arrived, John was in the emergency room on a gurney, with oxygen in his nose. After explaining who I was, the doctor in charge told me John's heart rate was 30 beats a minute. I watched as they placed a device on his chest. I was later told, "Anything below 30 beats means you are dying. We hooked him up to an external pacemaker to see if we could get it beating faster." Several times as he lay there a Heparin shot was administered, then some Glucagon to reverse beta blockers. I stayed out of the way as they seemed very focused on keeping him alive.

Two hours after my arrival, Dr. Evangelistia stepped over to me and gave me an update. He had called Dr. Chen, John's heart doctor, and explained John had a high degree of AV blocks in his system and that he needed Coumadin to thin his blood. He was prescribing a new medicine, Amlodipine once a day. He ushered me to where John lay and showed me the external pacemaker.

"We are admitting him to the cardiology unit. If this is just a problem with his medicines, he will probably go home tomorrow."

John lay on a gurney and once again I followed him down halls and in elevators to a hospital room. All through the evening and into the night they worked with him, trying to get his heart rate higher. At one point I heard the word arrhythmia. I was uncertain what was happening; however, I was very aware he was not okay. Early the next morning the hospitalist, Dr. Gawlik, came by. As I asked my questions, he told me John had been in very critical condition but seemed to be doing better. Even though that was good news, Dr. Gawlik made it extremely clear John would not be going home soon.

CHAPTER THIRTEEN

John experienced a consortium of doctors as they made their rounds May 1st. At 7:41 Dr. Gawlik came by with more questions as he studied John's heart chart. Next was Dr. Chen at 8:30. "Your heart block is gone, and you can go home. But you will need different medicines." Dr. Arif showed up at 12:45 and pronounced, "Everything looks good, Boss. I will prescribe new meds and you can go home."

But all was not well. His heart rate was jumping from 59 to 76, then falling even lower and then even higher, leaving him feeling very fatigued. His blood pressure was way too high, so he was given an anti-anxiety shot.

He was not going home after all.

Next day an EKG was taken. Dr. Gawlik said, "There is some concern about what is going on. Your blood work is good, but your heart is not functioning okay. You were in 1st degree AV block when you came in. We still need to make sure that doesn't happen again."

5/2/13 – to John from a friend.

"Just heard you were in the hospital. How are you doing? Can you have visitors?"

"I'm doing fine. No real need for visitors. They are just monitoring my vitals to make sure the new medicines are working and I'm stable. Of course, I've never been stable before."

On the 3rd, his blood pressure was too high and his heart rate was 133. His blood sugar had maintained around 250. As the day progressed, I heard words like conversion and flutter. He was finally diagnosed as being in atrial fibrillation, an abnormal heart rhythm. That afternoon Dr. Chen came by. "We may have to do ablation if your left atrium is the right size." All his words were entered in my binder to research later.

While John slept, I responded to a text from another friend, questioning why he hadn't been told of the hospitalization. "John has said to tell no one, so I haven't. I'm sure sorry. Feel free to tell him what you think about not knowing. He's been in the hospital since Tuesday morning, but he may go home today."

Next text was directed to John:

"Way to go!!! No one to look after Joy or Charlie. Wondered why we didn't see you last night. Don't be like me. Let somebody know what's going on."

"It was a heart rate issue. It was 27 when I came in due to some medications I'd been taking. Now it's up to 100 and they're trying to get my medications straightened out. I was planning on going on the ride tomorrow, but probably won't since I'm still in the hospital."

"27 not good. 100 not good. How about 72? Let them take care of you."

"I am, but I don't have to like it. I feel like I'm incarcerated but with good looking jailers."

While all this was going on, John continued speaking with his dentists. They had his cell phone number and had no idea he was lying in a hospital bed.

On the 4th, Dr. Chen came by. "We have you stabilized. Your left atrium is normal, so we could make ablation work. I've contacted Dr. Ravi in Spokane regarding performing the procedure. You can go home today."

I've heard that before. I'll believe it when I see it.

Dr. Tandon (from Dr. Arif's office) ordered blood work to check on his creatine. "I'll put a STAT on it so we should have the results in thirty minutes. If your creatine is okay, you can go home."

Dr. Gawlik came by. "We will check your Coumadin levels. If they are okay, you can go home."

I felt like saying, "Promises. Promises."

Finally, the assortment of physicians agreed, John could go home. As I had observed these doctors up close and personal for several days, I became aware that each doctor viewed John from the perspective of their specialty. The cardiologist looked at heart rate and pumping capability; the nephrologist examined his kidney function. Each individual area of John's health had to align before the discharge.

A nurse placed John in a wheelchair and pushed him to the sidewalk. Then she looked at me and said, "You can go get the car and pick him up." He stood from the chair and said, "Oh, no problem. I drove myself here" and walked away.

The look on the nurse's face was priceless. I shrugged and headed to my car.

Five days later we were in Dr. Chen's office.

"Your heart rate is 56. If you are in AFib it will bounce around. I'm starting you on Dilacor. It can be prescribed two different ways; a powder or granules and the other way is small tablets, which come four to a capsule. I'm prescribing the tablets. Pull the capsule apart and take only two. That's for your blood pressure. I'm also prescribing Clonidine, one tablet at bedtime for the next five days. This, too, is for blood pressure. You need to check your blood pressure at least twice a day. If the top number is over 200 or the bottom number is over 115, check again in ten minutes. If it is still too high, go to the ER. Go back on Benicar and stop the Amlodipine. Change from Furosemeide to Torsemide. Don't take any more Lipitor. Come back in one week. I will send a copy of your blood work to Dr. Arif."

I felt like I needed to attach the binder to my hand. I could never remember all these details without help, and they changed so often.

The next day we received a phone call from Dr. Chen. "Increase the Torsemide to twice a day. I still have concerns about your heart rate. You are weak from your stint in the hospital. We will continue watching the swelling in your legs, which needs to go down."

Now that he was taking Coumadin, it was required for him to have regular blood clotting checks. His number was a little high, so they upped his medicine. "Never eat grapefruit and don't take antibiotics. Come back in a week and we'll keep working on it until we get you stabilized." As we left the clinic, I thought *now he's on blood thinner. I wonder if that will affect him taking motorcycle rides. If he had an accident, he could bleed to death. That's a discussion we'll have later.*

Next day he received a text from Pastor Phil:

"John, how are you doing?"

"Doing a little better. I still have some weakness. I went to work today and worked most of the day. Big mistake. I'm kind of tired now."

Two days later, John made a stop at an Urgent Care as he made his delivery rounds, just a small fact he didn't share with me at the time. They told him he needed to see his kidney doctor, so John called Dr. Arif. "I'm just too fatigued. I can't function."

"Boss, I think you are allergic to Clonidine. Don't take it anymore. Double your hydralazine and reduce your Torsemide to once a day. Watch your blood pressure. You should start feeling better when it is 150-160 on top. When you start feeling better then you can tweak your medicines."

That same day, Dr. Chen called John. "I've talked to Dr. Arif. I will let him regulate your blood pressure medicines. Go with the changes he suggested. When we get your INR stabilized (the coagulation factor) then we will do a cardioversion and arrange for a consultation with a cardio physicist. Come back in one month."

I was in so far over my head, I felt like I couldn't breathe. John's life depended on us getting all this correct. *Dear God, please clear my mind and give me wisdom to understand all these instructions.*

It was time for a break from all the heavy stuff. We took a day trip to one of our favorite places, a cabin at Tollgate owned by one of our Starbucks friends. We spent several hours strolling by the lake, walking through the trees and sitting on the patio. There was still a lot of patchy snow on the ground. On our way home, we topped our breather off with a hamburger and shake from Ice-Burg in Walla Walla. This much needed time had allowed us to be almost normal, holding hands and laughing.

It was time for a party. One of our Starbucks Gang was moving away, so John and I planned a goodbye sendoff. Thirty-eight friends joined us to wish her well as she left for the next chapter in her life.

The next day was our 33rd anniversary. I had requested Outback to celebrate, since I love a good steak. He took me to Costco, took my picture eating a hot dog and then posted it on Facebook. Here's what he said: "Took my wife out to eat for our 33-year anniversary. Getting older is fun. No high expectations."

Comments on his post:

"Big spender."
"Did he use the excuse again - I forgot my wallet?"
"Throw caution to the wind. Nothing but the best for Joy."
"Our 43rd is coming up. I think I'll try for Costco."
That was on Saturday. Sunday, he took me to Outback.

CHAPTER FOURTEEN

A t our next visit with Dr. Chen, he presented me with a new diagnosis to enter into the binder, acute bradycardia. When I asked exactly what that meant, he explained: "He has an abnormally low heart rate. This causes organs to become oxygen deprived. It can lead to confusion."

"What about aggressiveness? Agitation? He's never yelled at me before, but when I bent over to help him he swatted my hand away and shouted at me to leave him alone."

"Sounds like he's having a reaction to the Percocet or Valium. Don't give him any more of either of those."

A few days later we met with Dr. Kneller, from Spokane. He traveled to the TriCities once a week to perform his specialty, ablation. Another new word. I was learning more than I ever wanted to know.

"Cardiac ablation is a procedure that creates scar tissue in your heart to block some of the electrical signals and is used to restore normal heart rhythm. I've looked at your reports. You need a pacemaker first, then maybe three weeks later the ablation. I would make a bridge of your tissue and that should stop the flutter. I checked about doing a cardioversion next Monday in Spokane, but the insurance won't let me do it that fast. My plan would be cardioversion, then pacemaker, then ablation."

I listened in awe as Dr. Kneller talked. This was an actual human being speaking with such a robotic voice and absolutely no inflection that I may have missed some of his words. My brain was busy trying to compute this was a live person. He asked for an EKG and when it was completed, he reported back that John's heart rate was bouncing between 31 and 50. "My office will call you to schedule the ablation after your cardioversion and pacemaker."

Cardioversion is where they use paddles to stop the heart and hopefully it restarts and goes back into rhythm. This procedure had been done to John once before several years ago. I had been in the room and watched as his body bounced off the bed and he made strange sounds, just like on TV. In his compromised state, I wondered at the wisdom of stopping his heart, but I was no medical expert. John didn't seem to be bothered. He spoke of it in computer language, "Just a reboot."

John was on a regular schedule to have his blood checked every month for the clotting factor. The goal number was between 2.0 – 3.0. Too much coumadin could cause massive bleeding and not enough could lead to blood clots. Several times since he started having it checked, it had dropped to 1.4, and down to 1.2 once. They kept working on adjusting his medicines. Then the number went too high, over 3 and once over 4. It was like walking a tightrope.

With all this going on, he continued to ride the motorcycle. *He gets so excited when a trip is planned. It's wonderful he's able to keep on riding.* He had friends who accompanied him equipped with an emergency kit in case of an accident. Before he left for a trip the next day, we discussed the issue of bleeding.

"Do you worry about me when I leave on a motorcycle outing? My friends can help me if I'm bleeding on the outside, but if the bleeding is inside, there's nothing they can do. I would probably bleed to death before help arrived."

Such comforting words.

"John, I know how much riding means to you. When you leave, I put you in God's hands. If it's your time, there is nothing anyone can do, and you will have died happy. But I'm always relieved when I hear the garage door going up and the motorcycle pulling in."

On June 12th, Dr. Ness called. "The insurance won't let me schedule a PET scan, so I've arranged for a CT scan on the 20th, but no contrast. Never have a contrast scan, ever. If something shows up, then we can do a PET scan. Get your blood work done before the scan."

Father's Day weekend found us headed back to John Day, Oregon, but it was different this year. John was too weak to navigate the twisties, so a good friend volunteered to bring the emergency kit and ride with him on the slab. I had the tent set up and ready when he arrived. He climbed off the bike, crawled in it, and slept until evening when we all gathered around to tell tall tales. The next day he had to say goodbye to his friends as they headed to Dooley. He just wasn't up to it. He slept most of the day but was waiting to hear their stories when they returned. Once again, a friend followed him home, ensuring his safety.

Back home, it was time to resume the doctor and scan routine. A CT scan was done on his abdomen, neck and chest. We would be told the results later.

One day, as John made his dental rounds, he stopped for lunch at the deli in Yoke's. When he entered, he spied a table occupied by four Pasco policemen. Deciding this was his opportunity to give them a hard time, he strode to where they were sitting and said, "Which one of you guys gave my wife a speeding ticket when she was hurrying to the hospital because I was in the ER with a heart rate of 27? She told me she explained her need for speed but was given a ticket anyway."

The culprit either wasn't at the table or he lied. But they apologized and explained to John I should have appealed. Too late. It was already paid. My focus that day had been my husband, not paperwork.

We had been instructed to be at the hospital at 6:00 am on the 24th for his scheduled cardioversion at 7:30. We arrived at 5:45, but no one showed up until 6:00. We were taken to a room and his vitals checked. His heart rate was 32, blood pressure was 191/76 and his oxygen was 97%. They placed an oxygen tube in his nose and hooked him to the machines. I watched his numbers on the monitor and noticed his heart rate went as low as 30 then up to 31-32. I began praying. *God, I don't think this is going to work. As low as his rate is, if they stop his heart, it might not restart. Please help the doctor make the right decision about whether to continue.*

When Dr. Chen walked in and saw John's heart rate, he canceled the cardioversion. "You need to be admitted to the hospital. Your heart rate is too low. You need a pacemaker right away. We'll see if we can get that done in the morning."

The room they had planned to use for the procedure was in the Clinical Decision Unit, which was considered a short stay room. There was no bathroom and only a hard chair for me. I spent the day with John, crocheting and talking, but went home for the night.

A text John sent to a friend:

"So, Jim, it looks like I want to grow up and be just like you. I'm getting a pacemaker put in tomorrow."

Jim: "Where are they doing this?"

John: "I think somewhere in the region on my chest near my heart."

Jim: "That's not what I meant."

John: "Got to have a little humor about this. Actually, I'm in Kadlec Hospital and not exactly sure what time they are going to do it. Probably tomorrow afternoon and then I go home on Wednesday."

Apparently, John liked that line because he tried it again on another friend:

"So, Charlie, it looks like I want to grow up and be just like you. I'm getting a pacemaker put in tomorrow."

Charlie: "What time? Where?"

John: "Kadlec. Don't know what time yet."

Charlie: Thanks for letting me know."

Another one to Charlie the next day:

John: "Dr. just came by and said surgery will be at 5:00 tonight."

Charlie: "Thanks, John. I'll let others know and pray for a successful outcome."

John: "Thanks."

Charlie: "Are you getting bed sores yet?"

John: "I'm tired of being in bed, but no bedsores. I appreciate the prayers. I will be kept overnight."

Charlie: "Did they ever stop/start your heart? What room are you in?"

John: "No, they did not do the reboot. 1114"

John had eaten a grilled cheese yesterday at 4:30, but now was on clear liquids. Charlie and Jim came by to visit. While they were with him, I took a break and went to lunch. About 3:00 they moved John to a much nicer room on the cardiac floor. It had a couch and a bathroom with a shower. I helped him clean up, then dashed home to get stuff for me to spend the night. While I was there, I made arrangements for someone to take care of our dog, Charlie.

John was taken to surgery at 5:15 and was back by 7:00. He hadn't eaten for over 24 hours, so he was very hungry. I hurried to get him a chicken quesadilla and Dean brought him a root beer. We didn't get much sleep that night, due to lots of alarms, beeps, and nurses. And there was a big change in John's appearance. He had now been shaved on the left side of his chest, which meant he was no longer lopsided.

After surgery:

Me: "He's back in the room. Thanks for the prayers."

Charlie: "Is he awake? Thanks for the update."

Me: "He's awake, eating and ornery."

Charlie: "Great news. We have an awesome God."

Next day: 8:12 am

Charlie: "How's the patient?"

Me: "He's in X-ray, but he's been up and had a latte. Doing good."

John sent a text to his brother: "Getting out in a bit. Things are working very well."

CHAPTER FIFTEEN

June 26th, I was awakened at 6:30 am when a man walked into the room carrying a small machine about the size of a laptop. He pulled John's bedside table over to where he stood and placed the equipment on it. As he opened it up and began to push buttons, I asked, "What are you doing?"

"I'm just checking to make sure his pacemaker is working correctly."

I watched in amazement as he manipulated John's heart rate. I could see on the monitor as he lowered it and then made it go high. More clicks of the keyboard and he informed me he had programmed the pacemaker for a heart rate of 70. He factored in a lower and higher rate, but anything too low or too high would set off an alarm. Fascinating.

"Can I have one of those so I can control him?" Laughter.

Dr. Chen came by to complete a final check and impart more instructions before discharging John. "Go take a walk and let me monitor how high your rate goes." After we took a stroll around the hall, he said, "That made it go up to 108. That's good. At noon, take your dose of Coumadin and resume your regular medication schedule. You can sleep on your side. I've given you an arm sling to wear until Monday and then you can take your arm out. It needs to remain immobile until the lead wires attach securely inside the heart. Do not raise your arm on the incision side for ten days. Be sure and take your temperature every day. We will be checking for infection. You now have to carry an ID card. Do not go through any metal detectors, not even hand-held ones. This pacemaker allows MRI's. Carry your cell phone on the opposite side from the pacemaker. Avoid magnets. Avoid strong electrical fields

– ham radios – leaning over the open hood of a running car. One side effect is hiccups that won't stop."

That was a lot of rules to remember. And sure enough, the hiccups returned. But the promised discharge occurred. Guess who drove us home.

I had made plans months before to attend a writer's conference in Portland that weekend. While Dr. Chen was in John's room. I had asked about leaving John alone, and I received the needed permission. Later that evening I shared, "I'm going to have a hard time leaving you for the conference, but honey, I need a break. Talking about writing will give my mind a different focus for the weekend." He totally understood and sent me off with his blessing. It was not an easy decision for me, and I received a lot of flak from some attendees when they found out what I had done. But all was well when I returned home, refreshed and ready to handle more.

I received a text at 4:15 pm:

Charlie: "Are you home? How is it going?"

Me: "No. He's driving us to the store."

Charlie: "Praise God. Glad all is well. Our hearts are in sync."

Of course, he drove us to the store. He was like the Energizer bunny.

He spent those first few nights back in the recliner with me beside him. Since he was not a very compliant patient, the sling only lasted twenty-four hours. As he recovered, he mowed the lawn and took motorcycle rides. The pacemaker had given him his life back. There had been weeks when the trip to Banff, Canada had seemed an impossibility, but now he oozed energy. We began making our plans.

John called Dr. Chen just to make sure he could do things like take a gondola ride to the top of an 8,000-foot mountain. We were going to take advantage of many adventures while in Canada. The doctor gave the green light. "Go and enjoy."

But first we had to make the doctor rounds again.

Dr. Ness explained, "There was a technical problem with the CT scan, but I see no evidence of meaningful growth. The renal mass in your right kidney is more of a fuzziness. The likelihood of this being anything is very minimal, it's just some shadowing. I will request a PET scan again, which will give us a more detailed picture of what's happening. Call me the last of July and we will make an appointment for the first week of August." He also scheduled an appointment with an Interventional Radiologist, Dr. Kasthuri, whatever that was. We would figure it out later.

Next was Dr. Arif. "Boss, your kidney function is still only 35%. Make sure you drink enough water. I've called the radiologist. He thinks the lymph node in your kidney is pressing on the tube. We may do a biopsy, and you may need a stent placed in your ureter. I think we need a PET scan instead of MRI. The PET scan can look for nodes."

At home, we discussed the shadowing in the kidney. "You had that fuzziness yesterday and we didn't know it. Today we do. But since we have no idea what it is, let's go to Canada and leave that issue in God's hands." And so we did.

On the way there, we stopped at Radium Hot Springs and spent some time in a huge hot tub, more like a swimming pool, with a lot of other people. The scenery alone was breathtaking. As we drove, we passed mile after mile of spectacular mountains. We spent one day walking on glaciers. We took a gondola ride to the top of Sulphur Mountain, an elevation of 8,041. We experienced an unbelievable week and declared that trip was one of the highlights of our travel life.

John had been told several times he needed to drink more water, but he didn't like water so struggled to comply. We bought various brands. When he rejected them, we gave the unwanted bottles away. Then he discovered Propel flavored water. We should have purchased stock in the company. He bought it by the case...all flavors. Any time you saw John, he had a bottle of Propel in his hand. He was now consistently drinking the recommended water.

On July 30th he underwent a PET scan.

The first of August we were back in Dr. Ness's office. "It seems you have a mass in your right kidney causing compression. I've spoken with Dr. Chen and have his okay for an MRI, but I think we need a biopsy first. I can't tell if it's lymphoma. I'm just not sure, but the biopsy will tell us. Dr. Kasthuri will perform it. There are four very small spots in your lungs. The procedure will cause pain and bleeding, and perhaps infection. It will form a hematoma since your kidney has lots of blood vessels. If you don't hear from Dr. Kasthuri by Tuesday, call me. We need an appointment in two to three weeks. Call the day before the appointment to make sure the pathology report is there. If it is cancer, we will make plans to remove your kidney."

We were composed as we possibly faced cancer again. John held my hands and said, "Honey, this is not our journey. It's God's, and He knows what He's doing. There's a purpose for this path we're on. I just want others to know Him and if it takes this journey to be able to share with them, then it's worth it. We don't know the result, but either way, it's okay."

Our peace remained.

On the 9th of August John had an appointment at Columbia Interventional Radiology Consulting with Dr. Kasthuri. I looked it up to see what Interventional Radiology was. It is a sub-specialty of radiology, and the purpose was to determine the cause of the shadowing.

I wrote more instructions in the binder as he talked. "Stop your Coumadin for five days. You need to get there forty-five minutes early to do INR testing. The procedure will take about thirty minutes and the recovery time requires at least one hour. Don't eat or drink anything after midnight the night before."

Five days later, we returned to the cath lab for testing, and then to Dr. Kasthuri. "I will make a minimally invasive incision in your kidney. With a small instrument I will push a catheter through your renal tube, through the blood vessels, and internally excise a small piece for biopsy."

Once again, I waited while he worked. But I was never alone in those moments. I could feel God's presence as He held me close.

When the procedure was completed, we walked to our car and went on with our lives. Even though a lot rested on the results of the biopsy, we didn't talk about it much. We had done our part; the doctors had done their parts and the rest was up to God.

CHAPTER SIXTEEN

O nce again, we were busy on Lorri's birthday. That's the day we went to Dr. Ness's office to be told the results of the biopsy. We held each other in the parking lot before entering the building. "We've faced down the elephant before. We can do it again." With a hug, kiss and holding hands, we were ready to find out.

"Well, it's not lymphoma, it is renal cell carcinoma. Kidney cancer is curable. You just remove the kidney, although removal of a kidney carries a great risk. It might require dialysis. That will be a question for Dr. Arif. You also have four spots in your lung. The kidney removal would not address them. We need to find out what they are. Let me call Dr. Kasthuri and have him look at the pictures of the lung nodules."

We waited while they consulted. When he returned, he reported, "They are too small for a biopsy. You need to see a urologist for kidney surgery. I recommend Dr. Salazar or Dr. Vance, but Dr. Arif needs to be involved."

Kidney cancer.

I can't imagine what it's like to tell someone they have cancer. And to think Dr. Ness had to do that on a regular basis. It takes a special person to stay as wonderful as he was while dealing with potentially terminal patients.

A text sent to our care group that evening:

John: "The diagnosis is kidney cancer. Consultations with other doctors pending. Treatment plan pending. Prefer to keep this quiet for now. At peace."

Jeanne: "Ed and I will keep you in our prayers. May our precious

Jesus send the Holy Spirit to lift both of you up physically, mentally and emotionally."

Juanita: "You're both in our thoughts and prayers. We love you guys. Please let us know if you need anything."

Brad: "Thanks for the update. We will continue the prayers with focus on the kidney. God is good all the time."

Tamie: "Please know we are praying for both of you. We love you so very much."

That Sunday we stood before our church and updated them on our journey. We remained in a cocoon of peace that passes understanding. As we shared, I could see the concern and caring on the faces in front of us. Oh, how I longed for them to believe that we did, indeed, have peace. Romans 8:28 tells us that all things work together for good to those who love God and are called according to His purpose. We felt our journey was part of His purpose.

Next was our visit with Dr. Arif. "Boss, your kidney is only functioning at 35% now. Many people don't know they have kidney cancer until it's too late. You found out way early. It used to be we took out the whole kidney when there was cancer. Now, we can take just the part that contains the cancer. When we remove that, the other kidney will enlarge to take over the job. Dialysis is needed 10-15% of the time. I will consult with Dr. Vance and see if he does laparoscopy. Then we will check with Dr. Ness to see if you need more chemo. You need another PET scan for your lungs in three months. Come back and see me in two months."

We needed a break from this medical merry-go-round, and we had just the solution. Our special group of business owners that we met with annually were gathering in Boston this year. We loved Boston and made plans to attend the meeting. Tickets purchased, bags packed, we made our way to the airport. Old hands at this traveling stuff, we placed our carry-ons in the bins and headed for the metal detectors.

And then it was time for a comedy routine, not exactly the optimal place to have one.

When they motioned for John to move forward, he walked through the machine, and it went nuts. Suddenly, a cacophony of sounds emanated from the apparatus. We looked at each other, What in the world was going on? Oh, we had forgotten John had a pacemaker. Security took him aside and it was kind of fun to watch as they practically stripped him naked searching for the offending culprit. Fat chance they could find it since it resided inside his chest. He told them, "You're not going to find it. I have a pacemaker." They handed him his pants, he retrieved his wallet from the pocket, removing the ID card that proved he did, indeed, have a pacemaker. After he dressed and was released, we continued to our gate. Good times.

Upon landing at Logan Airport, we hailed a taxi. When we arrived at our destination, we gathered our suitcases and walked to the lobby of our hotel. John reached in his pocket for his phone. It was gone. He ran to the curb to see if the taxi was still there. No such luck. Apparently, it had fallen from his pocket as he sat in the back seat.

We checked into our room and called the cab company. They could not assist us, so we walked to a nearby AT&T store to get a new phone. As we progressed down the street, I noticed we were in the area where the Boston Marathon took place. Soon, we were passing buildings that were boarded up. Then we saw the yellow line across the street that stated it was the end of the race. Lots of memories flooded back as I recalled what happened on that spot the previous April.

What a wonderful weekend. We laughed and ate and walked and ate. Well, you know what it's like. Enough meetings were thrown in to call it a business trip. At the end of the final meeting John asked for a few minutes to speak. Tears rolled down everyone's cheeks as he spoke.

"This will be my last DLOBA meeting. I've been diagnosed with kidney cancer. I don't know all the details yet, but my kidneys are already compromised from years of being diabetic. And there are spots in my lungs. I just want you all to know how very much I love you. Meeting with you every year has always been a highlight. This wonderful weekend is now in my memory bank. Joy and I will miss you."

One of the hardest speeches I've ever listened to.

One week later we were in the office of Dr. Vance. My second binder was getting full, and I was pondering the need for a third one. I mentioned to Dr. Vance that Dr. Arif wished to consult with him. I also asked if he did laparoscopy, and would this require more chemo?

"I prefer to open up instead of laparoscopy. I ice the kidney first to help control the bleeding. If I do a partial nephrectomy, you would be left with 60% of your kidney. But you may still need dialysis even with just a partial. Sometimes the dialysis is short-term until the kidney function returns. Your creatine levels have improved. There is a huge difference in recovery time between laparoscopy and open surgery. You will be in the hospital for three to five days and will have a pain pump. You will need to be off your Coumadin for two weeks. But first, before we do that surgery, you need a stent inserted to improve urine flow."

An appointment was scheduled with Dr. Vance for the following Tuesday as a pre-check before the surgery. "Before I place the stent, I will shoot some dye to see the extent of the blockage. It will be done under general anesthesia, but the recovery time is quick. And you need to do blood work before it. I recommend Dr. Jim Porter in Seattle for the laparoscopy. "

As the days passed, John began to find pictures on his phone of beautiful women. When he showed them to me, I gave him a hard time. "Hiding something from me?" Then family photos showed up. Soon he had a whole portfolio. He took his new iPhone to the AT&T store and explained what had happened in Boston.

"Someone found your phone and they are now using it. When they take pictures, you receive them. Do you want that to stop? I can turn the other phone off and it will be dead." John gave his assent and it worked. No more pictures.

On the 20th John underwent an EKG, chest X-ray and blood work in preparation for the stent surgery. It was news to me that you could even put a stent in a kidney. I was beginning to understand the body is a machine, and all these various doctors were just in charge of different pieces. I laughed at John's response when we talked about it. "Parts are parts."

September 25th John received a new part in his body, placed there to help drain his kidney. After surgery, Dr. Vance told us, "I discovered you have chronic kidney disease. Your kidney is very long, so the initial stent wasn't long enough. I didn't have a longer one handy and we had to go looking for one. But it all went well."

We returned home for him to recover from one more surgery.

That Saturday morning, we climbed in the car and headed to Starbucks. Some time with our friends was just what the doctor ordered. As we chatted, I watched a motorcycle friend enter and walk to John's side, leaning over and whispering in his ear. John's face morphed into shock and pain; the color drained from it. He made eye contact with me and tipped his head toward the door. I followed him outside.

"Joy, I was just told Dick (another motorcycle friend) was killed in a motorcycle accident last evening. He was only two hours from home after his trip to California. Apparently, he slid on some gravel and collided with a semi head on. I just can't believe it. I need to go home."

That news affected John in more than one way. He had taken many trips with Dick, a fellow off-road rider. Dick had been in our home attending the motorcycle parties and we had been a guest in his. But John's pain went deeper than that. Dick was not a Christian. John was beating himself up for not being more fervent in his attempts to share about Jesus. His failure weighed heavily on him.

CHAPTER SEVENTEEN

Barry and Diane, some very good longtime friends from out of state came to visit. Their concern for John was evident and it was so wonderful to see them. Barry and John had been the ones to start the business group, DLOBA. That was to be a temporary name until the group was organized and voted on a name. But it stuck. Dental Lab Owners Business Association.

A few days later we invited some friends, Steve and Deb, for dinner. John sent Steve a text:

"Will we see you guys Friday night?"

Steve: "Talk to your wife. We're in. What can we bring?"

John: "I talk to my wife all the time, so what's your point? You can bring yourselves but appreciate the gesture."

Steve: "Deb said she accepted with Joy last Thursday. We would love to come."

John: "Apparently my acerbic wit didn't come across."

The same day he sent a text to Lorri:

"A box arrived at our front door today. I was forced to eat it all. Thank you so much. Burp."

Lorri: "Glad the box arrived. Happy Bach house, including Charlie."

More friends, Moe and Sandi, from out of town came to visit, also concerned about John. We had a very nice time. They, too, were longtime friends in the dental business.

To celebrate Hanford's 70th anniversary, a tour was given of the B Reactor and T Plant. John had not been able to take a previous tour due to his compromised immune system and it seemed really important to him. Once again, I stayed up until the wee hours to sign up before the tour was full. It was a fascinating few hours, but he did end up exhausted from repeatedly climbing on and off the bus.

On the 18th of October, John was on the phone for 1 ½ hours trying to schedule an appointment with Dr. Porter in Seattle. He was supposedly going to do the laparoscopy surgery on John's kidney. John spoke with Michelle who transferred him to Ashley who transferred him to Janice where he got an answering machine. He left a message. "It's been two weeks since the nuclear renal scan and we have received no feedback from Dr. Porter. We need to schedule the surgery. Please call us."

Janice called right away. "We have not received any information regarding a John Bach needing surgery. Before we can do anything, we need a report."

John called Lourdes Hospital and found a person who told him the report had been sent two weeks ago. I called Dr. Porter's office and asked what their fax number was. Then I called Lourdes to confirm the report had been sent to that number. It was. So, they sent it again. Dr. Porter still did not receive it.

I was through playing that game.

John called Dr. Vance's office and asked if they had received the report. They had. So, they sent it to Dr. Porter, who received it. Finally. The next day we received a phone call from Dr. Porter's office requesting John have blood work done and another CT scan when he arrived in Seattle.

We needed a break, so took a day trip to Walla Walla where we held hands as we strolled through the town. We ended our trip with a hamburger at Ice-Burg, complete with not a shake but a malt. Yum.

And now it was November.

John had an appointment with a radiologist at Swedish Hospital in Seattle on November 12th. He was to receive a CT scan of his chest/abdomen/pelvis searching for renal cell carcinoma. We left town on the 11th to arrive in Seattle in time to have dinner with our granddaughter at 5:30. We headed for the timeshare at the Camlin at 6:30. Due to side effects of some of his medicines, John could not control his bowels, so we had learned to carry extra clothes. He had a bad accident before I could help him to the room. I left the car in the parking lot without paying in the box so I could get him upstairs and cleaned up. Bless his heart. He was so humbled. And in my mind, I thought, *I'm watching him revert to childlike accidents.*

When I went back to the car, I planned to pay and then unload the car. As I went around to the passenger side, I hit my head so hard on the mirror sticking out from the big truck beside us that I saw stars and had to hang on to the car. *If I pass out down here, what will John do? In his weakened state will he come looking? Of course he will.* When my vision cleared, I spied a ticket under the windshield wiper. Close to tears, I paid the tab in the parking lot box, got our suitcases and returned to our room.

I was ticked. I called the number on the ticket and talked very forcefully to the man on the other end, who passed me up the line to someone else, who passed me up the line to his supervisor. John was grinning as he watched. He knew I would not give up. Finally, it was resolved, and the charge reversed. Yay for me.

We had to pay $10 to park at the hospital. It's a good thing we arrived early because there was more than one elevator and you had to be on the correct floor and get on the correct elevator to arrive at radiology. His appointment was at 1:30 and they took him back at 1:51. The recommendation was that John receive a robotic assisted partial nephrectomy (removal of his kidney).

Next was Dr. Porter's office where there was a lot of paperwork to complete. We were finally ushered into his office at 3:30. A Fellow, Stepanian, came in to get more information before Dr. Porter's arrival at 4:00. "I have the results of the CT scan. You have new and enlarging pulmonary nodules in your chest since July 30th. I am suspicious for metastatic disease, with progressive endobronchial inflammatory process less likely. Some of the nodules do have an endobronchial distribution. *Does he have any idea we don't understand what he's saying?* You have a large tumor on your right kidney and spots on your lungs. Your abdomen shows an enlarging mass at the lower pole of the right kidney, decreased right hydronephrosis with the stent in place and cholelithiasis. (I asked about that. Gallstones. Why couldn't he just say it?) Surgery may not be the way to go. The mass is unusual, in the center right over the blood vessels. So, I can't do a partial since I can't separate the tumor from the vessels. The only way to stop the kidney cancer is to remove the kidney. The problem is the cancer is in your better functioning kidney. If we remove it, the other kidney cannot perform the needed job. You would have to go on dialysis. The lumps in the lungs may not be big enough to biopsy, but we need to know what they are."

How does a wife process information like that about the love of her life? We held each other close that night and drove home in the morning.

At our next appointment with Dr. Ness, he and John spent some time talking about where all of this was going. John said, "Dr. Porter made it clear that to stop the kidney cancer, that kidney needs to be removed. Then I would need dialysis. I just want to let you know, I do not want to go on dialysis, to be hooked to a machine. I understand it might prolong my life. But what about the quality? I intend to live with cancer as long as I can and then accept the outcome. I'm not afraid to die."

When John made that statement, Dr. Ness looked at me. I knew he was wondering if I approved. "This is John's body and John's decision. I am here for him, whatever he decides." Dr. Ness nodded.

But there was also good news. November 16th, we received a phone call from Tammi telling us she would be coming for Christmas. Very thoughtful and something to look forward to. Lorri had already made plans to come. The family was gathering.

CHAPTER EIGHTEEN

Going to Seattle used to be for pleasure. Never had we traveled there so often and for such various medical appointments. John's lung biopsy was scheduled for November 20th at 10:00 in the morning, and he was to have nothing to eat or drink after midnight. We drove the three and one-half hours the night before and checked in at our home away from home, the Camlin, a condo arranged for us by Lorri.

This time we entered a different parking garage which was attached to the Main Swedish Hospital. The rate for this one was $24. Signs for Radiology directed us to the East elevators, 4th floor. The new name to place in my binder was Dr. Feldman, Radiology Specialist. He was a very nice man, soft spoken and welcoming.

"I will go in through your back. Most of the nodules are very tiny. The largest one is on the left side. I will be watching closely for bleeding or an air leak. If either of those become an issue, we will keep you overnight in Short Stay."

They took John back at noon. I walked to a hallway of full-length windows with a panoramic view of Seattle spread out before me. *Dear God, be with the doctor as he performs this biopsy. Guide his hands. Protect John. I know this is part of your plan, but I don't like it. It seems he's gone through enough. And what if more cancer is discovered? I give all of that to you. I can feel you here with me right now. Why would I think you would leave me? I'm so grateful for your love and for our peace. Help me be what John needs as we take this journey.*

When the biopsy was completed, Dr. Feldman came to talk to me. "I gave him the same drug that is used for colonoscopies. He will be in recovery for an hour while we monitor his blood pressure. Then we will do another X-ray to see if there is any bleeding."

Since I didn't want to drive after dark, I asked, "Will he be able to drive tonight?" The doctor said he wouldn't recommend it. So, I began checking the motels in the area by the hospital. We had been told if you explained you had someone who was a patient in the hospital, they would give you a discount. With the discount, the one directly across from the hospital was $209 a night. I called a motel down the street; $235 a night with discount.

I was finally allowed into the recovery room and stood by John as he lay on the table. Dr. Feldman came by. "All is good. No air leaks. No bleeding. You will be discharged. Dr. Ness will have the results in two to three days." I explained my findings regarding the motels in the area. The doctor said John could probably drive home but repeated he wouldn't recommend it.

John drove us home. Of course he did.

Dr. Ness called the next Tuesday. "John, the biopsy shows you have renal cell carcinoma in your lungs. I'll want to see you in my office after Thanksgiving." We also received a phone call from Dr. Porter confirming the kidney cancer had metastasized to John's lungs.

But life went on. That Friday evening, we held our annual dessert social the weekend before Thanksgiving. By then, word had gotten around about John's diagnosis. Fifty-two friends came to love on us and laugh with us. They had now heard John say more than once, "I'm not dying from cancer...I'm living with it." That's what we intended to keep on doing. Our peace reigned supreme.

Once again, we packed the car. But this time we headed the opposite direction to Boise. We were spending Thanksgiving Day with John's daughter. We checked in to a motel close to her house. There were shops and restaurants nearby, so we did a little strolling around when we got to town. As we walked and talked, suddenly the topic changed. "How do you feel about cremation?" I never knew when something like that would come up. It was evident he had been giving it some thought. "I'm not against it. For me, the grave is not where you will be, so I'm not sure I would be going there. If you want to be cremated, then we'll arrange it."

On the first of December, my very loving and caring husband came home with an early birthday present for me...a Keurig. I'm sure the look on my face said it all. *So, you bought yourself a present for my birthday?* I don't drink coffee. Don't even like the smell. Yet, here was a way to make a cup any time I wanted one. He did some stuttering and stammering as he explained he was sure there were other drinks available for the Keurig. I forgave him. He could use it and we could have it available for our parties. Later, I discovered chai tea.

On the 4th of December, a very important meeting was held. We needed to sell our business…a business John and a partner had originally built from scratch beginning in March, 1986. It had necessitated a move from Boise to the TriCities. We had lived and breathed teeth for almost thirty years. I watched John grapple with the knowledge that he could no longer be a major part of the company. His stamina level just would not allow it. But this was his baby and he wanted to hang on as long as he could.

One of the members of DLOBA, Skyler, who lived just across the border in Idaho had attended the meeting in Boston where John had said he had cancer and it would be his last meeting. Sky had begun examining avenues to ensure he could make the offer to John to buy the lab. He now had all his ducks in a row. He came to town, we took him to lunch, and the dialogue centered around the details of that transaction. Skyler assured John his baby would be in good hands and the plans were put in motion.

For my birthday on the 5th of December, John announced he wanted to take me to Spokane to celebrate my birthday with our friends there. That was unusual, but these days I just went with the flow. Upon arriving in Spokane, the true reason became evident. John drove straight to downtown, parked in a garage, took my hand and led me to the Apple store. By the time we entered, John was so fatigued I asked that a chair be brought for him. *I wonder what piece of technology he doesn't have?* I would soon find out.

He had me stand in front of him, took both my hands in his and said, "Joy, I want you to have a good setup for your computer and iPad for when I'm gone and won't be here to take care of it. This buying trip is all about you. I love you and don't want to leave you, but it seems that is the direction I'm going. So just let me do this for you without arguing."

How could I argue? I couldn't even speak. Tears ran down my cheeks. He was thinking of me as he faded away. We hugged and cried in front of God and all the clerks and customers, and we didn't care. I left the Apple store with a new iPad and a very large monitor. I had been unaware they made them that big. "Honey, I know you want to write books, and your eyesight is failing. I'm hoping this monitor will help you accomplish your dream."

I was overwhelmed with his display of love and caring. How could I give him up? God was definitely going to have to provide the courage and grace for me in the days ahead.

Two days later, the Oakridge Boys Christmas Show was at the Toyota Center in our town. It was their 40th anniversary tour. John really wanted to attend. He rested most of the day. Then he got up to get dressed in time to leave but was too weak. Just one more thing we missed.

Our appointment with Dr. Ness on the 10th resolved any questions we may have had about this journey. "Your cancer is no longer curable. It will be several months before symptoms begin. *You mean he hasn't had symptoms yet?* We will start some new medicine in January after your different insurance is available. Some of the medications are very expensive, so we may need to request help from the drug companies for co-pay. I would say you have six to twelve months, but with the pills it may be longer. You no longer need to take the Coumadin. Soon you may begin to have shortness of breath. We will do some blood work and another CT scan the first of the year so we can embark on your new treatment plan."

At home, we sat at the dining room table, trying to absorb all we had been told. John asked, "So how do you feel about me dying?" That is not a question I expected to ever hear from my husband. It seemed surreal. But we had always been honest with each other.

"I don't like it, but it's hard to see you like this. I've read the stories of someone walking into the hospital and shooting their loved one in the hospital bed. I'm beginning to understand that. If I could make it better for you, I would."

"Should I worry?"

And then laughter. We had God's peace and each other and all was right with our world.

CHAPTER NINETEEN

Christmas was coming. We were hosting a motorcycle Christmas party, so it was time to decorate. In our previous house, our Christmas village had filled the living room, wall to wall. But in this house, the focus had been changed to nativities. As I placed them around the rooms, I prayed for the party, for the fellowship and for John's strength to be able to enjoy it.

John wanted a Christmas tree for when Tammi and Lorri were here. We hadn't had one since the very first year in this new home when John purchased an artificial one tall enough for our vaulted ceiling. He had even done all the decorating, a one and only time. So, I was a little surprised when he suggested getting a tree, but we didn't go all out. It was small enough to set on a table. He had an agenda I didn't know about.

After he rested, we went shopping for presents for the kids. Our tradition for Christmas was to make plans for a nice trip for the two of us sometime in the spring, so we never bought each other gifts. Unbeknownst to me, as we shopped, he was keeping track of items I commented on. We returned home and I was wrapping presents when he said he had an errand to run. He went back to four different stores and bought me presents he knew I liked.

Lorri arrived first and a few days later Tammi came on Christmas Day, so our Christmas Eve was on the 25th and Christmas morning was the 26th. Lorri and Tammi had placed their gifts under the table where the tree was, so I did not notice any extras. Imagine my surprise when the gifts were handed out. I gathered quite a pile in my lap. I had nothing for John and he had four for me. He immensely enjoyed pulling one over on me.

But life with cancer continued.

A CT scan without contrast was performed on his chest, abdomen and pelvis which obtained 199 images. The findings: interval development of multiple bilateral pulmonary nodules in the left upper lobe. The right middle lobe contained a conglomerate mass. The right lower lobe was comprised of adjacent nodules in a vertex. Calcified stones in his gallbladder, calcifications in lower pole of left kidney and a mass arising from the anterior inferior margin to the right kidney appears to show increase in size.

This was mostly just words to us. We knew the journey we were on. These big words didn't change that.

The last Sunday of the year, we were asked to speak at church once again. We shared the truth we had been told and the peace that was real. John said, "I'm not afraid of death, but I have to tell you I'm a little concerned about the process."

And then 2013 was in the books. Only one and one-half years ago, life had been simple and predictable. Now it was complicated and unpredictable. As we communicated our thoughts and feelings, we agreed that this walk through a terminal illness had caused us to grow exponentially in our Christian faith.

Side note: When we were building our new home, we considered installing a hot tub on the back patio. We had several friends who had stopped using theirs after a few years, because the upkeep was just too much trouble. So after much deliberation, we decided to put a jetted tub in our bathroom. Very unexpected to me was John's need for the exact tub he wanted. Our builder and friend, Tyson, framed in a tub. John climbed in and back out. "No, not big enough." Tub #2 was the same procedure. We even traveled to another house being built by Tyson and John climbed in that tub. "No." Tub #3 required some adjustments to the framing before it could be brought in.

"This is it," Tyson told John. "I can't get any bigger than this."

John climbed in, then motioned for me to climb in too.

"Are you crowded?"

"Well, John, since I have all my clothes on, plus my shoes, I don't think this is a good try-in. But it's up to you."

We kept #3.

Little did I dream how very important that tub would become. As his illness progressed, John got colder and colder. Eventually, the only way he could truly get warm was to get in the tub immersed in rather warm water. But it also became our sharing spot. He talked to me more in that tub than he had ever talked anywhere else in the house. I treasured our moments there. So, when I say we communicated our thoughts and feelings, we were probably sitting in the tub.

The second day of 2014 we were in Dr. Ness's office. "I've seen the CT scan. Your cancer is very aggressive. There are two ways to go, a chemo IV or chemo pills. The pills are very expensive, but the IV has more side effects. You may begin to experience chest pain, a cough or shortness of breath. That's because your lungs can no longer function normally. We can radiate your kidney if needed. I will check out your insurance and see if it will cover the pill. Come back in two weeks."

Two days later found John at Design Dental Lab in final negotiations for its sale, which I found out about later that evening. I was puzzled he hadn't mentioned it to me so I could be there. I think it was just too painful for him to end his business career and he didn't want me to witness it. We were dealing with much bigger issues, so I worked through my feelings without discussing it with him.

Two more days passed before we received a phone call from Dr. Ness. "Your insurance company denied coverage of the pill. So, I'll request coverage for a different prescription. This one has some side effects such as serious liver problems, it turns your skin yellow and can cause heart problems including death. *Really! So, no problem.* One month supply costs between $9,000 and $12,000. I've checked with a foundation that has approved payment beginning in February."

His words left us stunned. Side effects including death? But he was dying any way so that wasn't as big an issue as the cost. $9,000 to $12,000 a month? We could never afford that. Thankfully, Dr. Ness had gone to bat for us.

Another two days and John sent a text to his accountability group:

"Sorry, won't make the meeting tonight. I'm pulling together everything for the sale of my lab tomorrow."

And then it was done; the papers signed. What a poignant moment, bittersweet for me as I was not a part of it. Design Dental

Laboratory was no longer ours. It had been a thriving business that kept us fed, clothed, sheltered and well-traveled. John was only 67. He had always said he would keep on working until he died, but he had been talking about old age. This was not the way we had envisioned the end of ownership.

But we experienced blessings along the way. Trigg, a good Starbucks friend and my hair stylist needed a place to live for a month. When I told her she was welcome to stay in our extra bedroom, she hesitated. She knew John had cancer and didn't want to be a burden. Plus, she explained, she also had a dog, a Shih Tzu. John had allergies, but Shih Tzu's were okay. When she moved in, we didn't know each other very well. But by the time she moved out, she had become like another daughter and her dog, Vivien, a constant companion to John. Our dog, Charlie, was too big to be a lap dog, but Vivien fit very nicely. We considered both of them a bonus in our roller-coaster life.

This is what John wrote about that time:

A few years ago, we built a new house. One of the important things we wanted was a guest wing where someone in need could come and find refuge for a while. We built that wing and various friends and family slept there, but a few years passed before it could be used for that purpose.

Then one day we had the blessing of a friend who was in need. She didn't want to be a bother but needed a place to stay for a few weeks while her condo was being readied. So a smile came to live with us for a while.

The smile was a little tarnished and cracked by life and it was small, but it remained here with us. The smile spent time with us sitting in the TV room watching the Olympics together. We talked and laughed and the smile began to relax. Days passed, cookies were made and fudge consumed in amazing quantities, and the smile got bigger.

The smile was going through some tough times but talked little about her emotions. We hurt for her but could only offer our hugs and company. We prayed for her every day that she would find peace and comfort. As the days passed, we laughed more and more and came to know what a kind and loving person this smile was. She was moving into our hearts as well as our home. Then came the day when her place was nearing ready to move into and my wife and I talked about what a hole it would leave in our hearts when the smile moved out.

Well, the day came and the smile was ready to leave but an amazing thing happened. She left but the smile stayed in our hearts. Now we understood why all those years ago as we designed our new house that guest wing was so important to us. You see, in both of our lives we had needed a refuge at one time, and we could now pay it forward. We learned that the smile helped us as much as we helped her.

Thank you, smile. We will always love you.

CHAPTER TWENTY

O ur car knew the way to Dr. Ness's office. When we began this journey, we had no idea the magnitude of what this doctor would contribute to our ease as we traveled. We trusted him explicitly. He was a direct answer to one of our prayers and we listened carefully when he spoke.

"Your insurance has approved the chemo pill to help extend your life. The co-pay is sometimes $2,000 up to $4,000. We'll see what we can work out. Your blood work looks good for the upcoming treatment. The numbers tell me that we can start in two weeks. You will take one pill a day for four weeks, then off two."

We were ready for this next phase.

We received a text from Paul Null:

"Wow. Just listened to your testimony. WOW! Again! Peace to you dear brother and sister."

Me: "Love you."

John: "Love you too."

On the 24th, we received a message from Dr. Ness's office. "The Foundation will pay the co-pay."

Another answer to prayer.

One of the presents John had given me for Christmas was a plush floor-length bathrobe. I sent him a text at work as I got ready for the day: "Every time I put on my robe, I feel wrapped in love."

"Points?"

"Yep."

"Smile."

Two weeks after John took the first chemo pill, Sutent, he underwent a consultation regarding it with Leila at Dr. Ness's office. His report to her: "I have diarrhea, redness in my hands and feet, and some discomfort."

"Sutent is an oral biological agent, a targeted chemotherapy. The side effects are more tolerable than IV chemo. Take one at the same time each day for four weeks. If it upsets your stomach, take it with food. I will give you a prescription for nausea. The pill may cause fatigue so rest as needed. If you get too tired to get out of bed, call the doctor. Avoid strong smells, spicy or acidic foods, and foods may taste different. You may need to take Prilosec. If the diarrhea continues, push fluids. Your skin may turn yellow. Don't take any hot baths. With the pain and redness in your hands and feet, avoid playing the guitar. *Really? The guitar?* We will watch your blood pressure and may need to change your dose. Call us if you get a cold with fever over 100. Avoid trauma. Continue to use the Cerave lotion. Let us know if you feel achy. Having cancer puts you at risk for blood clots."

Now we were into February.

John sent a text to Tammi and Jim:

"Thank you very much for the CD. I love it. Very thoughtful of you."

"So glad you like it! We thought of you when we saw a concert of them on TV."

John wanted to take one last trip. On the 8th, our friend and travel agent, Pam, brought information to our home and we sat around the dining room table. John had told her he always wanted to take an Alaskan cruise, so she was prepared to share about that. But the more he questioned her, the less he liked the idea. Too much time was spent out in the ocean and not enough time exploring on land. I had never wanted to take an Alaskan cruise, but it really didn't matter to me. It was far more important that he went on the trip he wanted. She began to spread out brochures and information about a paddleboat up the Mississippi. Astonishingly, John was immediately hooked. As we talked, his enthusiasm increased. It was perfect. Pam would do her research about dates and get back to us.

Four days later we were in Dr. Ness's office. John told the doctor he had lots of gas and heartburn. "Eat Activia with probiotics. Keep using Tums. You can use Prilosec if you want, one tablet a day as needed. You can exercise if you feel up to it. According to your last blood test, the medicine is affecting your thyroid. Your TSH is high, so I'm adding a prescription for that. Take it fasting first thing in the morning, then wait before you take your other meds. We will get a scan again after you take three rounds of the chemo pill. I will call seven to ten days in advance to arrange for the next dose."

As John's caretaker, the dispensing of his pills was my job. I purchased several types of pill holders and carefully focused each time I filled them. He was now taking fourteen tablets and capsules a day. The astonishing thing was he would put the pile in his hand and take them all at the same time. Unbelievable.

On the 20th, John was not waking up, eating or drinking. His temp was 100.9. Through the day, he did not improve. I knew if he wasn't better by morning, we would be taking another trip to the hospital. Sure enough, his temp was 100.7 the next morning, even after taking two Tylenol. He was admitted to Trios with severe dehydration, and I had a new name to enter in my binder, Dr. Kinder. Nice name. After a brief two-day stay, John was discharged.

A few days later his hands began peeling but were no longer painful, and his energy seemed to be returning. He had reached the end of the four-week cycle on the chemo pill, and it was time for the two-week break. He continued to try to work, but now he wheezed in the mornings. He would go to work and be back home in two hours with no strength. Each breath, his lungs made funny noises. We just lived with it.

Over the years, John had shared with us his dream of being able to speak German. At one point he had hired a local German woman to teach him. He had traced his lineage back generations and believed he was descendent of Johann Sabastian Bach, who had twenty children. Since John now had some extra time at home, Lorri purchased the German Rosetta Stone program for him. The look on his face when he opened the box was priceless, like a little kid who just got a bicycle. When he was rested, he would head for his computer and learn a little more. The program spoke the word, so he could know how it was supposed to sound. And so did I. Whether I wanted to or not, I was learning German. I recognized the noise the computer made when John did not pronounce the word correctly. He was a determined student and spent hours in his office with a grin on his face.

A text from Lorri:

"Have fun Dad – Love you – Are you fluent yet?"

John: "See Mann isst – Der."

Lorri: Wonderbaar – Guten Nacht, Papa."

John: "Guten Nacht mudchen – spellcheck doesn't do a good job mit German."

Lorri: "I noticed. I understood what you meant. So glad you are enjoying your present. Happy early Father's Day."

John: "Ja"

Lorri: "Guten tag."

John: "Go to knock. I was trying to say good night, but boy did that get translated wrong"

Lorri: "The phone doesn't speak Deutsche – Guten nacht – Dad – ich liebe."

John: "Same to you."

Time seemed to be flying by. March had arrived already. I was fascinated as I watched John's pacemaker be checked remotely. He was part machine. Apparently, it was working just fine.

On the 11th, it was time for his next round of the chemo pill, but he had to pay a visit to Dr. Ness first. "Your thyroid is okay. You are still anemic and may need a blood transfusion. Start the chemo pill tomorrow and come back on the 24th to check your blood work and see if we have your meds correct so you can take your trip."

The paddleboat company, American Queen, had requested a letter from Dr. Ness basically wanting him to guarantee John wouldn't die while onboard. With the letter, we would be accepted as passengers. We all smiled as we discussed the absurdity of the request, but Dr. Ness wrote one.

Another party was in order before we left. We had now lived in this wonderful home for four years. Thirty of our friends helped us celebrate.

One more visit with Dr. Ness. "Your anemia has improved, so no blood transfusion for now. Your thyroid has been altered and I need to adjust the prescription. Take two pills instead of one. Your creatine level is off, but Dr. Arif is out of town. Go see him when you come back. After your trip, I will need to see you, and we'll do a PET scan. Keep track of your temp while you travel. You may need to see a doctor while you're gone."

We left Dr. Ness and drove to Pam's office to pick up all the required paperwork for our trip up the Mississippi. On to our big adventure.

CHAPTER TWENTY-ONE

March 29th our daughter, Lorri, traveled from Georgia to spend her week of spring break with us. We always loved her visits; lots of fun and laughter. The 5th of April came all too quickly.

Our thoughts turned to the mighty Mississippi River. John wrote in his travelogue:

"Packing (gathering) suitcases. Is this one too big? Too small? Did I remember to pick up the clothes from the cleaners? Do I have all my meds? (Getting old, you tend to carry a pharmacy.) Does our house sitter have all the contact numbers? Does the dog have enough food for two weeks? I feel an attack of ADHD! Do we have all our paperwork (including the letter from the doctor) for the ship? My wife checks again for the fourth time. Okay. I think you get to a point packing where you walk around the house with a blank stare and look at your suitcases and say, "well if it's not in there we'll figure something out", and then my wife checks the tickets and cruise ship packets for the fifth time. Off to the airport. Wait. Let's check the paperwork one more time."

This time, at the airport, we remembered John had a pacemaker. Things went much smoother.

We didn't exactly take a direct route to New Orleans. John wanted to visit his family in Illinois first. We landed in Springfield, rented a car and headed to a motel. Soon we had a gathering enjoying pizza and stories. The next day we headed east to visit some of his lifelong friends. It's hard to say goodbye anyway but knowing it's the last time you will see these folks makes it even tougher.

A few days into the trip, John took his last chemo pill. That would help him feel better for the rest of our adventure. We drove through six states from Illinois to New Orleans, taking a slight detour so I could add one more state to my list of states I've been to. Our car was a Ford Fusion, and when it was time to buy gas, we searched high and low for a button or lever to open the gas tank. No luck. Finally, we drove to a Ford dealership, but the salesman was no help. We watched as he tried all the same tricks we had. Another customer on the car lot overheard our dilemma. He walked to the car, placed his hand on the gas cap, gave a little push and the cap sprang open. Slightly humiliating, especially for the salesman.

Before we entered New Orleans and began that part of our trip, I requested we drive a little east and cross the longest continuous bridge in the United States passing over water…the waters of Lake Pontchartrain. For eight of the twenty-four miles you can't even see land in any direction. Quite unbelievable.

There had been a slight mix-up in our plans. We won't say who had made the motel reservations, but we were going to be short one night; the first one. And New Orleans was already flooded with people coming for the various music fests that were happening. To keep John from absolutely panicking, I had to spill a secret. Lorri was already there, having driven from Georgia to spend a few more days with us. She had a room, and some unexpected roommates. All was well.

John ordered pecan pie ala mode from room service. Pie $8, ice cream $3, delivery charge $3.50, service charge $2.31, tax $1.64. Total - $18.45. He enjoyed it! As a diabetic since 1983, he had forgone so many treats, it was fun to watch him dig in.

Music oozed from every nook and cranny of the French Quarter. In one more week, the annual Jazz Fest would be in full swing. We lunched on a patio and listened to a band in a park across from us. As the three of us walked up and down each street, music was offered on the corners and sometimes a band would march down the sidewalk. What fun. John and I held hands and grinned.

He loved seafood; and New Orleans was definitely the right place to enjoy it. Lorri and I abstained from those specials and opted for hamburgers and salads. We watched John in amazement as he ate his fill of lobster, oysters and gumbo. He relished the plethora of tastes available. I tried a beignet but did not finish it. Lorri and I just enjoyed the music as we observed John's delight. A few months ago, everything had tasted like cardboard to him. He deserved every delectable morsel.

One morning we climbed aboard a swamp tour boat to visit the alligators. There were plenty of huge ones along the bank. We had our pictures taken holding a baby alligator.

One week ago, Lorri had left our home in Washington to return to Georgia. Now we had already seen her again for two days in New Orleans. Surreal. We built memory on top of memory, to replay in the coming days, feeling blessed beyond measure. Goodbyes were shared once again, and we watched her little blue car disappear into the traffic as she headed home.

By 3:00 pm, it was time to gather our luggage and embark on this next big adventure. We would be aboard a paddlewheel steamboat complete with steam calliope. As we boarded, John and I discussed the age group of our travel mates. In our 60's, we thought we would be among the oldest. Boy, were we wrong. Wheelchairs, canes, and walkers accompanied seventy-five percent of the people boarding. We grinned some more.

The boat traveled by night so we could spend the day at our destination. Our first stop was Oak Alley Plantation. Twenty-eight 300-year-old live oaks lined the path leading to the graceful twin staircases that ascended to the front door. I could write a whole book about the history and beauty of that place. Of course, we had to try a mint julep. I voted no on finishing mine.

Next day was Angola Prison. Most of those prisoners will die there since there is no parole for condemned murderers. Angola has become their family, city and life. With good behavior, they can earn the privilege of living in dorms, dressing in jeans and white t-shirt and working on the grounds. At first it was a little unsettling to know the man holding the door open for me had killed someone. Intriguing day.

We received a text from Trigg with a picture of Charlie.

John: Thank you for taking such good care of him.

Trigg: My pleasure – Are you ready to come home?

John: No, we're staying for two more weeks.

Trigg: Good. I'm having fun in my pretend house, watching TV and eating you out of house and home.

April 15th was when I had a big surprise planned for John. We were to spend the day in Natchez, Mississippi, the home of one of John's favorite authors. Greg Iles just happened to have a new book coming out that day. I had seen the notice months before and been in contact with his office, explaining we would be in town. I was amazed at the response I received. Caroline, his assistant, made arrangements to meet us at the mooring with an autographed copy for John.

When our boat pulled up to the dock at 9:00 am, our conversation went like this.

"John, we need to get off now." (I had texted Caroline and could see her standing at the top of the ramp with a sign that said Bach.)

"No, I think I want to eat some breakfast and go into town later."

"John, we need to go now."

"I will in a little bit."

"You are going now."

"Why are you being like this?"

I walked him to the railing, pointed to the lady standing at the top of the ramp with the Bach sign and said, "Because of her."

"Why does her sign say "Bach"?

"Maybe you should get off and go see."

I enjoyed the next few minutes very much. He was overwhelmed. We hugged and had our picture taken with Caroline. He carried his treasure clutched to his chest for the next several hours.

Our next stop was the National Military Park in Vicksburg. After that came Baton Rouge, where we took the elevator to the top (27th) floor of the state capital. As we talked with the other couple in the elevator, we discovered they were from Australia and the man told us about sailing in the America's Cup yacht race the previous year. At dinner that night, back aboard the boat, our tablemate talked about his day visiting his good friend, Jimmy Swaggert. We met so many interesting people on this trip.

Our last stop was Plantation Road and then on to New Orleans. We had mixed emotions. It had been a blast, but not actual life. We had slept, eaten, seen things and visited with new friends, living the life of leisure. Reality was just around the corner.

CHAPTER TWENTY-TWO

John fell asleep before the plane took off. A plethora of wonderful memories flooded my mind. There's something to be said for listening to Moonlight Sonata while flying over clouds. Next, I was looking down on Kansas (that can be taken more than one way). Above Colorado I said "hi" to my brother down there. And it's never a good thing when the pilot tells the flight attendants to sit down.

I knew when we landed, the medical whirlwind would begin.

First it was blood work and a PET scan which turned into a CT scan. It was time to go back on the chemo pill. Two days later Dr. Ness gave us the results of the scans. "The bulk of the disease has not grown, except for one nodule in the lung. A new area is forming in the top of the left lung, but I believe the treatment is effective. Your kidney is still a concern. Come back in four weeks and we will scan again."

The first of May, John was feeling well. He loved the ocean, so we took a quick trip to Seaside, Oregon. We had been there multiple times and it was like a home away from home. We held hands, strolled around town and down the promenade. Known as the "prom", it's a mile and half long sidewalk parallel to the beach, giving him a chance to see and hear the ocean up close without having to expend the energy necessary to walk on sand.

"I think there's something wrong with my toe."

That was a new symptom. We returned to our room, he took off his shoe and sock, along with a complete toenail. I fixed him up with a large band aid and off we went again. This time, as we strolled, the conversation took one of those unexpected turns.

"Do you think you'll remarry? I don't want you to be alone."

"Babe, I've not given one second of thought to that. No. I won't remarry. I've had steak. Why would I want a hamburger?"

That comment elicited a grin.

After a quick visit with Dr. Ness on the 22nd, with only minor changes in his meds, the next day we drove to Boise, Idaho for John's grandson's high school graduation. Upon returning home, John began his fourth cycle of the chemo pill.

We had observed while in Idaho that all was not going well at John's daughter's house. His teenage granddaughter was struggling in school and at home. After much discussion, we offered to take her for the summer. John's annual Father's Day motorcycle rally in John Day, Oregon would be an excellent time to pick her up.

John was blessed with wonderful motorcycle cohorts. Since he was on blood thinner, they knew riding a motorcycle was even riskier than normal for him. But friends promised to ride right behind him, carrying the kit to staunch any possible bleeding. He didn't have the stamina to ride on the twisties for the trip, so once again they sacrificed that pleasure to ride on the slab. We placed the whole event in God's hands. It did my heart good to see the grin on his face as he left town. Of course, as the mule, I drove my car.

When the weekend was over, I had a passenger as I headed home; a very sullen, non-verbal traveler. But by the end of the three-and one-half-hour trip, we had come to an understanding. She could tell me her feelings and I would listen.

John had agreed to help with her need to attend online summer school and received an email from her remote school counselor:

"Hello there, I would recommend she take the following classes: English 9B, Earth Science A, Earth Science B, and Algebra 1A. Please let me know if I can help in any way."

John's response: "I am her grandfather and am helping her through the online school. It appears she is failing the courses right now and I am seeking some help to get her back on track. Do you have any suggestions?"

Even though it was probably his last summer on earth, he expended a lot of energy trying to help her. Toward the end of June, Lorri came to visit for a week, and took her turn beside the computer. As a teacher, she was more familiar with the process than we were, and she was a tremendous help.

John had one more CT scan and we awaited the results.

Lorri left on the 2nd of July. John was in Dr. Ness's office the next day. This appointment coincided with his birthday, so they presented him with a cupcake, candle burning, and sang happy birthday.

"On a scale of 1-10, how bad is the pain in your feet?"

"It's a 10", was John's reply.

Another prescription, this time for neuropathy in his feet. "If you are still in pain in a few days, then double the dose. Come back in two weeks and we will re-assess. You still need to stay on the increased thyroid dosage. Stop taking Tylenol and start with the Hydrocodone every four to six hours. Next time you need to start the pain medicine a few days before you begin the cycle of chemo pill. You are having a wonderful response to treatment. The spots in your lungs and kidney have diminished. You have proven the Seattle group wrong."

A week later John went to work at 7:00 a.m. but didn't stay long. He returned home at 10:00, shivering, and climbed into bed. He slept the day away, getting up only for bouts of diarrhea. Each day, he repeated that routine, gallantly leaving for work, returning within hours, heading for bed with his trusty dog by his side.

The sicker John got, the colder he was. Soon he was wearing sweatpants and a hooded sweatshirt in the house…the hood pulled up over his head. Even though the temperature on the thermostat was set at 78, he was still freezing. I purchased a wool cover to place over him as he sat in his recliner…still dressed in his sweats. He even had down house shoes on his feet, which had been a thoughtful gift from Tammi and Jim.

The only place he truly felt warm was in the tub, filled with very warm water. Sometimes he went there two or three times a day. He would describe it as finally being warm inside. He would motion with his hand on his chest and show how he felt the warmth radiating outward.

Just a word about Charlie. We believe he was an unexpected gift from a loving God for these days. He would wait patiently by the window for John's car to come down the street. When he saw the car, his paws would go up on the sill and the tail would begin furiously wagging. As soon as he heard the garage door going up, Charlie would barrel through the house to the back door. I loved seeing the joy in their eyes the minute they spotted each other. He barely left John's side, lying with him as he slept; John with his hand resting on Charlie.

We still had a teenager to attend to, but the burden of that responsibility soon fell on me. John needed to focus on his health; some days were better than others. On the 17th, we traveled to Dr. Ness's office for a checkup. All was going as the doctor anticipated.

When the arrangements had been made for us to take his granddaughter for the summer, John had promised a five-day trip to Seaside for her and a friend if she worked hard on her lessons. Within weeks, we were off to Oregon, the friend having arrived from Idaho. However, it didn't work out quite as John had planned. He was too sick to do anything with them, but he was determined to fix their breakfast before they left for the day. As he walked in the kitchen, yelling erupted with each step, due to extremely painful feet. Nothing more could be done for the pain, so we accepted the noise and didn't mention it. But my insides winced in empathy, as it was difficult to hear.

After breakfast we handed them some money for lunch, two excited teenagers who had never been to the ocean before, and they were off for the day. Then I helped John get situated in the recliner by the big windows facing the water, where he spent the day drifting in and out of sleep. Since his feet were so tender, he remained barefooted. On day two, he took his last chemo pill for this cycle. Hopefully, in a few days he would feel better. By the third day, when he walked not only did he holler, but his skin fell off in large patches the size of a silver dollar. Yet he continued to cook breakfast.

Back home, the friend's mom drove from Idaho to pick her up. Then it was back to Dr. Ness's office. After checking John's feet, the doctor agreed something needed to change in his medication. "I'm prescribing a lower dose, but also considering changing you to a different chemo pill for the next cycle. If the lower dose starts to do something to your feet, just stop taking it. Come back in six weeks."

Arrangements were made to meet John's daughter on August 15th at a halfway point so her teenager could return home. We had poured a lot of love and caring into her for the summer. Time would tell if anything had changed.

CHAPTER TWENTY-THREE

T he rest of August was fairly doctor-appointment free, with only one visit to Dr. Markle. It had been a year since John had seen his nephrologist, Dr. Arif, so September 3rd found us in his office. "You are doing fine, Boss. Check with Dr. Vance regarding the kidney stent. You need to do blood work one week before that visit. After the placement, you need to watch for odor from your urine because you might have an infection in the stent. Come back in four months."

A good friend checked in about our trip to Seaside.

"How was your trip? Enjoy the ride?"

"Did not ride the bike. Had an energy slump. Spent most of the time in a recliner. But the girls had fun."

The 18th, 19th and 20th we spent in San Diego with some of our best buddies, the DLOBA group. Tammi and Jim drove from Pasadena to join us for dinner. What a refreshing time. Lots of hugs and loves.

Home again, John finished the round of chemo pill and had more blood work done. Dr. Ness's assessment was, "Your kidney function is slightly less. You will be off the chemo pill for two weeks and we will do a CT scan prior to your next appointment with me."

Before this journey began, PET and CT scans were not in my vocabulary. Now they just rolled off our tongues like we were old hands at it. And then we reached another impediment in our journey.

John was chilling and we both knew the remedy for that was a soak in the warm tub. I filled it and helped him in. He slid down to where just his head was sticking out and we left the hot water trickling in, so he could stay warm. I sat on the edge while we shared our thoughts. Those moments were always very special.

When he was ready to get out, he could not. His arms were no longer strong enough to push him up, and I certainly couldn't lift him out. We had always left the water in, to help buoy him up, but I pulled the plug. My heart was breaking as I loved on him sitting there with the water (and his heat) draining. When all the water was depleted, I grabbed a stack of towels from the shelf. He leaned forward as much as he could, and I shoved a towel under his butt. I let him rest and we repeated the process until he was high enough to get his legs under him and sit on the side. His body heat diminished, he trembled as I helped him swing his legs around to the floor. I dried him, pulled some sweats over his head and on his legs. We hurried to the recliner where I turned on the heating pad and covered him with a wool blanket.

That's when keeping him warm really got serious. And bear in mind, I wasn't cold. I was roasting. I never mentioned it.

I purchased a down cover to go over the wool cover. After I would place the cover over him, every time, he would say, "And tuck it in around my feet", and make the motions of tucking. The tucking of the cover around his feet, totally enclosing them, is one of my most precious memories. I would kneel at his feet and hold them.

The vows said, "for better or worse, in sickness and health".

Later, we had a tough conversation.

"Honey, you can never get in the tub again. If you do, I will have to call someone to help get you out." He understood. One more thing was marked off his list of pleasures.

October 8th, he began the next cycle of chemo pill.

John wanted to visit his brother in Nevada one last time. Phone calls and texts were shared, and Jim said he would take care of all the arrangements. It was a short flight and Jim picked him up at the airport. But there was a hitch in the plan. Upon arrival in their home, John discovered he was allergic to their dog. His throat began to close and eyes swell shut. Jim pulled some strings and got John on an earlier flight back home.

John received a text from my daughter, Tammi:

"I just renewed your NatGeo. Now it includes digital. I'm sure you have the latest iPad and know how to do it, so enjoy."

"Tammi, thanks so much. I really enjoy those and look forward to going digital. You know I like to keep up on the latest technology."

"I know you are comfortable talking about your health and medical issues, so I want you to know I have faith and renewed you for another year!"

"Well then, I'll just stay around to read them all."

"Yes, I think you should."

"Looking forward to Thanksgiving with everyone, including Sarah." (their dog)

"Yes, even Sarah has Thanksgiving plans this year."

"Thank you for the wonderful card."

"You're welcome. Jim (her husband) and I think about you every day. Hope you feel better."

"I'll take that as an order."

Side note: After the incident with his brother's dog, we took precautions regarding where their dog would stay. Our plan was to keep Sarah in a separate room and not come in contact with John.

Another visit with Dr. Markle, and then Dr. Ness. Sometimes the back-to-back doctor visits were exhausting, plus it seemed John underwent an endless round of scans. *I am so grateful for our peace. God's got this. I can feel His loving presence.* Arrangements were made for another CT scan of his chest, abdomen, and pelvis.

On the 30th of October, John and I met with our longtime accountant. We owned the building our lab occupied, and we needed guidance in how to go about selling it. With tears in her eyes, she explained the reasons why we should wait until John died before selling. We left her office to return to our jobs. As I drove, my mind replayed the meeting. Advice was being given on the premise that John was actually going to die. Sometimes that was difficult to absorb. Just that quickly, I felt the gentle arms of Jesus as He held me.

The next week was an appointment with Dr. Ness to learn the results of the CT scan. "We are starting to see growth in the nodules. It's time to change your path. I want to try Afinitor next. It's a kidney-friendly chemo medicine. The mass in your kidney is larger now than initially. The lymph nodes in your chest have enlarged and the nodules in your lungs are growing. We need to check with your insurance and see if they cover Afinitor. If they don't, you may need to change insurances. AARP covers most and seems to be very good, so they would be my first choice."

A few days later we received word from Dr. Ness's office that AARP would not cover Afinitor.

A former employee volunteered to paint some accent walls in our home to help spruce it up. She texted John: "Hey, John, I know you aren't working full days anymore. I got the TV room cleaned up first, so if you need to come home to rest, you have a place to go."

A new symptom appeared, blood in his urine. Dr. Vance was the urologist scheduled to place a stent in John's kidney, so we called his office. He was on vacation; however, John was told to come in and the PA would see him. We were not impressed. It took 45 minutes before anyone acknowledged us and they seemed very disorganized. The PA gave John instructions about changing the stent every three months. Dr. Vance had never mentioned that, and it just didn't sound correct. *That would mean a surgery every three months.* She continued to speak as though he already had the stent.

"It's normal to have blood in the urine when you have a stent. The lab work shows no blood or infection. It could have become encrusted."

We walked to the front office and booked the surgery with Dr. Vance, scheduling it for December 5th. We planned to check with Dr. Ness first to see if he agreed for John to go ahead.

November 20th we were once again in Dr. Ness's office. John had a cough and pain in his temple, but this was a routine appointment before starting the Afinitor. Even though our insurance had denied it on the first request, Dr. Ness applied again, and it had been approved. John also wanted to ask about taking one more trip to the ocean.

"Start the chemo pill tomorrow. If you experience feet swelling, high blood pressure, fatigue or seizures call 911. You may have a rash, brittle nails, itchy dry skin, chest pain and inability to sleep. We will monitor your cholesterol, triglycerides and blood sugar and continue to measure your kidney function. A nodule is pressing against your ureter, reducing the flow of urine from your kidney to your bladder. That prevents your kidney from emptying completely. That's why you need a stent. I'll see you again before the surgery. We'll just have to see how you feel when it's time for the trip."

But life was so much more than rounds of doctor visits. Even though John's energy level was flagging, his zest for life was not. It was time for another party. Our annual dessert social was held on the 21st, with thirty-nine very special people here. We shared an evening of overeating, stories and laughter, with plenty of dessert to go around.

CHAPTER TWENTY-FOUR

T hanksgiving week the only medical interruption was an x-ray of John's chest and abdomen in preparation for the placing of the stent. Thanksgiving had always been his favorite holiday and since we understood this would probably be his last, we wanted it to be special. Lorri arrived on the Saturday before, since she had the whole week off from school. Tammi and Jim (plus Sarah) came the day before Thanksgiving. As John rested in the TV room, we made plans for a bountiful meal; turkey, lots of side dishes, my homemade rolls and more than one kind of dessert.

A long-time tradition of ours was to go around the table and each person say what they were thankful for. After we were seated, John stood and said he wanted to begin the sharing. He gave eye contact to each individual as he spoke of his love for them, what they meant to him and how proud he was of them. When he got to me, he looked at me briefly and then moved on. We all had tears as his voice broke several times. I managed to keep my deluge under control. If I started crying, I wasn't sure I could stop. *How very blessed we are to all be here together. I'm so thankful John is able to join us. What a wonderful memory.* We ate until we were stuffed and then ate some more. Later, he explained he just knew he wouldn't keep it together if he tried to talk about me. I understood.

Lots of leftovers were consumed. Sarah was in a room with a sliding door that faced the back yard which we left open enough for her to go in and out at will. She enjoyed romping in the snow since she did not have that opportunity in southern California. Games were played.

A jigsaw puzzle took over the table. Much talking and laughter. A very bittersweet time. The goodbyes were difficult.

Then it was on to the next phase of this journey with blood work and Dr. Vance on the schedule. The doctor had lots of questions about John's pacemaker and when he last saw a heart doctor. We thought we were ready. But Dr. Vance was on call that weekend and the surgery scheduled for December 5th was canceled.

John's phone was busy. A voicemail from Dr. Markle checking on him and making sure he had the x-ray. A call from Dr. Ness. "Your white and red cells are fine. The kidney is a little worse. I want to see you again next week. Dr. Arif is out of town, but I've left a message for him to contact me when he gets back. We need to discuss your kidney function."

On the 4th, John took his last chemo pill in that cycle.

That evening Dr. Markle called John at home. That's never a good sign. "Have Dr. Ness take a look at your chest x-ray before you have the surgery." John called Dr. Ness and told him. Thirty minutes later Dr. Ness called back. "Talks about your stent surgery have been canceled. There is something in your lungs. I need to see you tomorrow, but first I need you to have a CT scan."

Dr. Ness called early the next morning. "I need you to come in now. I was thinking about you last night. You have been diagnosed with bi-lateral pneumonia."

In his office, he continued talking. "I'm very surprised by the chest x-ray. There are Grade One complications. I'm putting you on an antibiotic and steroid (Prednisone) to decrease the inflammation. Your chemo pill is on hold for now. Since you are diabetic, you need to keep a close check on your blood sugar because Prednisone will affect it. No stent surgery until your chest clears up." Then he sent us to the hospital for a CT scan.

The snowball seemed to be rolling downhill faster and faster.

We went back to Dr. Ness after he saw the scan. "You definitely have bi-lateral pneumonia, which means you cannot go back on the chemo pill. Not sure what we did that's working, but you are stable and do not need to be admitted to the hospital right now. When you finish the antibiotic, then go to half the dosage of Dilacor but stay on the Prednisone. Dr. Vance had back surgery, so he can't operate on you now anyway. I want you to see a pulmonary specialist. Your blood work shows you are slightly anemic. Trios Hospital needs the x-rays from Lourdes Hospital for comparison."

But enough with the serious stuff. It was time for another party. Thirty-five of John's BMW motorcycle club friends gathered at our house for an evening of overeating, playing games, telling stories, and ending with the infamous white elephant gift exchange. It was just what we needed.

Another huge pleasure was removed from John's life on December 22nd. It was a day we had known was coming, but the actual event was traumatic. John sold his F650 GS motorcycle. We watched it go down the street, knowing he would never get another one. When I said, "Babe, I'm so sorry," he said, "I can't talk about it", and walked away.

He posted on Facebook:

"Well, closing one chapter of my life. I've been riding motorcycles since I was fifteen years old. My dad bought me my first one. Time to move on. The bike went to a good home in Walla Walla."

Here's some of the comments:

"From Lorri: "I'm sorry Dad. I know that must have been difficult for you. Thinking of you. Love you."

"Sorry."

"It was my honor to be one of the last to ride it before it left your hands."

"You are a great rider, John."

"Tough to see."

"I'm so glad I got to ride with you this summer. I know it's tough."

John: "I have to say there was a tear in my eye when I saw my bike ride away."

We moved from motorcycles to doctor visits. Dr. Ness had requested an x-ray of his chest front and side. "Your insurance deemed it medically unnecessary and it was not approved, so I can't compare x-rays. I'm keeping you on Prednisone. Your white blood count is high. We will go another two weeks and I will request another chest x-ray. If it is still not changed, you may need to contact a pulmonary specialist."

Soon, John began experiencing swelling in his feet and cramping in his ankles and hands. A phone call to Dr. Ness's office was responded to by a nurse. "You may need to go in through ER." We just waited it out and he gradually got better.

His symptoms eased enough for us to travel to northern Idaho for a weekend to attend a Christmas party given by the new owner of our lab. Our accommodations were in a beautiful bed and breakfast in Coeur d'Alene where we enjoyed fun and food with the employees of his lab. It was a wonderful break for us.

The day before Christmas, he suggested we go for a drive. My idea of a drive is one hundred miles on the freeway, but from past experience I knew his was different. They always involved a destination. This time it was Archibald's car lot. "I've always wanted a red Cadillac. Let's see what I can find." He had never ever mentioned wanting a Cadillac. We knew all the salesmen there and he was allowed to test drive several cars, none of them a Cadillac. That's when he spied a red Cadillac on the car lot next door. In the few minutes it took to drive there, I tried talking to him. I knew he was in no shape to be wheeling and dealing with a car salesman, but he stubbornly forged ahead, losing a lot of money on the car he traded in. And on top of that, he also purchased a two-year warranty. *Doesn't he realize he's probably not going to live that long?* As we transferred belongings from one car to the other, the grin on his face was priceless.

Immediately upon ownership, he bought Borla mufflers for said Cadillac. They were very loud. It had never occurred to me that someone who wanted a high-end Cadillac would want it to be noisy. I thought, *perhaps he's replacing the motorcycle sound, since he can no longer ride.*

Once again he turned to Facebook to share his news:

"Did you see what I got to replace my motorcycle?" – with a picture. "Santa left his sleigh at my house."

"It helps to see this subsequent post. My heart was heavy for you."

"Sweet ride."

"Whoa! Stunning ride."

"Wow."

"Wow. Merry Christmas."

"Wow. You must have been a good boy."

"Nice!!!"

From Lorri: "Merry Christmas, Dad. I love you."

"John, looks like you've been good. Merry Christmas to you and Joy."

"I like your sleigh, Santa."

From Tammi: "Nice car! Red cars are the best. Merry Christmas."

"Sweet."

"WOW! I must have been on his naughty list. I didn't get anything like that."

That same day he brought home a Rumba vacuum cleaner which he promptly programmed to run several times a day. Such fun when it got stuck under the couch and emitted strange noises. But he wasn't through. He made one more shopping trip and returned with a new iPhone 6 Plus for each of us.

Chemo brain.

CHAPTER TWENTY-FIVE

C hristmas was very low-key. Well, as low-key as it could be with a new (to us) red Cadillac in the garage. He proudly drove it to Starbucks to show it off.

One day as we sat at the table, John said, "Lorri has asked me to write her a letter before I go. I've tried my best to do it. The words just don't say what I want them to. I believe actions speak louder than words. What if I adopted her?"

Instantly, tears ran down my cheeks.

"Is that the response I can expect from her?"

"Yes. She has wanted you to adopt her since she was a teenager."

We turned to our Starbucks lawyer friend who began making the arrangements for when Lorri came home on Spring Break in March.

John called Dr. Ness's office and told them he needed to see the doctor sooner than the 8th of January. Blood work was ordered, and an appointment made for New Year's Eve. Dr. Ness came into the office just to see John, who told him, "My hand cramps are getting really bad, generally in the evening. My bowel habits are all out of whack and I feel like my breathing is different. My feet are also still swelling every day."

"Your blood pressure is up. Your kidney seems to be about the same. Go off the antibiotic but stay on the Prednisone. I am ordering a CT scan of your chest and abdomen – marked 'with urgency'. Double up on your Torsemeide for a few days. The foundation that has been providing coverage for your prescriptions has said they are out of funding for your specific type of cancer. I was given the name of another foundation, but they are out of funding also."

Later that day, Dr. Ness called with the name and phone number of a third foundation that might be able to help with the cost of his medicine. I could hear John's side of the conversation when he called them. "I will not mortgage my house and leave my wife in bankruptcy to get this medicine. I cannot afford $12,000 a month."

John never knew how that affected me. Making an excuse to leave the house, I drove to the river and sat in my car. I was so upset at the idea a pharmaceutical company could just blithely tell John to decide whether to go into bankruptcy for the opportunity to extend his life, that the sounds of my anguish filled the car. What kind of people calmly say, "pay or die"? When my reaction had run its course, I returned home, and we resumed our life.

New Year's Day John paced himself as he worked in the garage and bedroom sorting through his motorcycle gear. That afternoon he texted a motorcycle friend, "Hey, if you're around this afternoon and not doing anything, come on down to the house for a few minutes. I've got some gear you might want."

"How about Friday?"

"Friday or lunch some time will be best. I have a 10:00 am doctor appointment and a 4:00 pm CT scan, so somewhere in between."

"Headed down now."

On January 2nd, there was no office staff at Dr. Matharu's pulmonologist office, but he came in at the request of Dr. Ness to look at the CT scan of John's chest, abdomen and pelvis.

"This may be an opportunistic infection. You have sick sinus rhythm and atypical pneumonia. There is some fluid in your lungs, maybe mucous. The hand cramping is from the Torsemeide. Start taking Mag Oxide – three pills a day. There is a popcorn pattern in your lungs. May be metastasized. It's foggy around it, inflammation but absence of fever. Chances are low that it is pneumonia and high that it is the spread of cancer. I need to do a bronchoscopy. The results of that might change your therapy. You may have blood clots in the future and need Lovanox – a shot in your belly – once a day. Lower the dose of Prednisone you are taking to 10 in am and 10 in pm."

While the doctor talked and I was taking notes, it was hard to pick up on all the words as they went by. But I heard the sentence that said the chances were high that the fogginess in his lungs might indicate the spread of cancer.

John's bronchoscopy was scheduled for the 7th at 6:00 am at Lourdes Hospital. A nurse took him to surgery at 7:00. An hour later, Dr. Matharu came in. "The procedure went well, and he is in recovery. I did a needle biopsy of his windpipe cartilage, airway and lung and I think I got some good tissue. He may have a slight fever today and can take Tylenol for that. He may cough up dime to quarter size blood clots today, but there shouldn't be any tomorrow. I will try to get the results to Dr. Ness by tomorrow."

The next few weeks were a blur. John had an appointment with Dr. Ness, sold his motorcycle riding jacket, had blood in his cough, kept an appointment with Dr. Arif, drove to the car dealer and picked up the license plates for his Cadillac and met with a Realtor to begin negotiations about selling our business building.

We sat at the table where we could hold hands and look into each other's eyes. John had something on his mind. "Honey, I know you want to be in your room, writing. I'm so sorry you have to be out here taking care of me. I wish you didn't have to."

Does he even begin to understand how much I love him? "Babe, if it was the other way around and you were having to take care of me, would you be upset at giving up riding your motorcycle? This is not a sacrifice. I am willingly by your side. It's where I belong. And you know that in the future, I will have all the time I want to go in there and write. Please let me give you my love in every way possible."

He accepted my words.

We continued with our Saturday morning routine of climbing out of bed, pulling on some clothes and driving to Starbucks to meet with our "gang". I observed John as he drove…and wondered if he should be behind the wheel. I had never seen him go so slow, especially when he got to the roundabout. *We just might have to have another one of those serious discussions.*

A lady acquaintance was leaving as we entered, and asked him, "How are you doing?" His answer, "I'm outliving my expiration date." We always had a delightful time with our friends. They were very aware of John's health yet treated him just like normal.

As we walked to the car to leave, John handed me the keys and said,

"I should not be driving." Enough said. I now had keys in my possession to a car I had never wanted and found stressful to drive. But for the two months he got to drive it, the grin on his face was priceless.

A few days later found us back in Dr. Matharu's office. "Dr. Long, the pathologist, found renal cell carcinoma in your lungs, but did not see any lymphoma. We are still waiting for the lymph node test results. You do not have a fungus or virus. I am giving you an Albuterol inhaler to help with your breathing. Take two puffs up to four times a day. Just wait a couple of minutes between puffs. You can go back on the chemo pill. I've ordered some leg cramp pills for you."

The next morning, John took two puffs of the inhaler; and waited to get better. Several hours elapsed, then John took two more puffs, but his breathing became more difficult. By evening, we knew the inhaler was only making him worse. With a call to Dr. Matharu the next morning, the puffs of Albuterol were discontinued.

When the call ended, John looked at me and asked, "Is this the way I'm going to die? Not breathing?" My heart broke as I gathered him in my arms. "Honey, I don't know. We need to talk to Dr. Ness. I wish I could fix it. But I'm here…right here…for the long haul. I will do whatever I can. This seems to be part of the journey that we are on. And I know God is right here with us."

We turned once again to our core doctor, Dr. Ness.

"I can't breathe. My lungs feel full. I've tried sleeping in a chair, but I choke. My legs and hands are cramping and Dr. Matharu ordered some medicine for me, but I haven't filled it yet. I wanted to talk to you first."

"You need to start taking Afinitor for Friday and Saturday, but not on Sunday. Dr. Matharu still doesn't have the results of the culture, but I am in touch with him. You have a slight temperature. I'll call you as soon as I talk to Dr. Matharu. For now, don't take the pills he prescribed. We need to know more before we can address the breathing issue."

And so, we waited. John continued to struggle to breathe, describing it to friends as trying to breathe through a straw. It seemed our love for each other increased minute by minute, with almost continual touching.

Dr. Ness called with the results. "Dr. Matharu has diagnosed you with kidney cancer in your lungs. Dr. Arif says to stop the Dilacor immediately, but it takes up to forty-eight hours to clear the body. I'm putting you back on Metropolol twice a day and I want you on Afinitor. Your breathing problem is considered to be "acute" and came on quickly. Afinitor has an IV alternative and I'm working on arranging that. Let's start you on Thursday and then once a week after that."

John's coughing was non-stop. We longed to be close physically but couldn't lay together anymore. He coughed. We couldn't talk. He coughed. We held hands and loved on each other with our eyes. Daily we declared our love for each other. One would say, "I love you" and the other would respond with, "More".

Were we nearing the end? I felt every obstacle I had overcome in my life had been equipping me for this journey.

CHAPTER TWENTY-SIX

On January 21st, John received a text from the new owner of our lab: "I plan to come to Kennewick on Thursdays and would like to meet with you when I do."

"I am going to have to be out all Thursday afternoon as my doctor has decided I need to go on a chemo drip for my lungs. It looks like that will be an ongoing event every Thursday. But he said it should only take an hour, once we get things going. I will attempt to schedule those appointments early in the day so I can be here when you come."

The next day we met with Dr. Ness before going to Short Stay for the chemo IV. In response to John's question about a new chemo pill, Dr. Ness said, "No, we aren't going to go back to a pill." John's intense relentless coughing had now produced a hernia, so a suppressant was prescribed. Then we moved on to Short Stay. The room was very cold with a chair that would not lay down all the way. He could not get comfortable and coughed the whole time.

A text from the new lab owner asked him how it went.

"Went really well. I was able to change my chemo dates to Wednesdays from now on so I can meet with you on Thursdays."

But he never bounced back from the chemo IV. His fatigue was overwhelming and going to work was not an option. He slept in the recliner, not even wanting to eat. "It all tastes like cardboard."

It became very difficult for John to stand up after going to the bathroom. In talking to Tyson, I learned there was such a thing as a toilet safety frame. It could be hooked to the toilet and had arm rails to help those in a weakened condition. I called Bellevue Healthcare. They delivered the frame the next day; Tyson stopped by and installed it. John was so grateful.

January 28th we were once again in Dr. Ness's office, the pre-visit before more chemo IV. "Your white cell count is very high. You have thrush in your throat from the Prednisone. I'm hoping we can go with at least a month or two of treatments before stopping the IV. If we find no benefit from them, there are alternative oral treatments available. John, I will do whatever you say."

John asked, "What is the point of chemo?"

"To prolong your life."

"Isn't that just prolonging the inevitable? I may not continue the chemo."

Hard words to hear.

Dr. Ness quickly looked at me. I said, "It's John's body and his decision. I will support whatever he decides."

John asked, "What about death. What happens?"

Again, Dr. Ness looked at me. So, I asked, "He has cancer in his lungs and kidneys. What is the difference in the dying process?"

"If the kidney cancer is what he dies from, it will be quick and painless. The electrolytes go out of balance and the potassium gets too high. His heart stops. If the lung cancer is what takes him, it's not pleasant. Basically, he will drown because he will no longer be able to breathe."

How can I hear these words and know they are talking about my beloved not being able to breathe? How am I going to be there for him?

Sitting in that chair in the doctor's office, I once again placed the whole situation in God's hands. Peace flooded me as I felt the assurance I wouldn't be alone. God's arms would be around both of us.

We held hands as we walked from that room, down the hall, into the elevator and to the infusion center for the next round of chemo IV. This time he was given a room with a bed, so he slept as the drug dripped into his body.

That evening, as we conversed about our day, John looked me straight in the eyes and said, "Babe, you will never know how much it means to me that you are letting me make these decisions about my health without any drama. I so appreciate how you are handling all of this. I can never thank you enough. I've lost control of so much of my life, at least you are allowing me to maintain dignity in my end-of-life choices."

My love for him welled up from deep within. "Honey, you are certainly managing your end of this crisis with a great deal of dignity. I have never loved you more. With your behavior, you are demonstrating to others how to die. You are a powerful witness to the presence of God in your life. I'm so proud to be by your side as we take this journey."

The very next day it was time to visit Dr. Markle again. He ordered a change in John's insulin to Novolog from Lispro and up 50 units for the Lantus, with instructions to come back in a week.

Over the next few days John's cough loosened and he gained some energy. But then he would have a horrible night when he couldn't breathe, and we would get no sleep.

On the 4th of February, we met with Dr. Ness before the chemo IV appointment at 12:30. The doctor said, "John, you are in no condition to undergo more chemo so I'm canceling it. It seems we may have to switch back to the Afinitor. You have some left from before, so start that today. You need to get an appointment with Dr. Arif to check on your kidneys. Come back next week."

This merry-go-round of doctor visits was exhausting. Next was Dr. Markle's turn again. "John, your blood sugar is out of whack. There is a sudden difference in your numbers because they canceled the chemo IV, so you need to cut back on the Lantus."

John related how hard it was for him to breathe. "I feel like I'm trying to breathe through a straw. I just can't get enough air."

"There's a name for that. It's called air hunger. The solution is for you to take Morphine."

"I don't want to take Morphine. I don't want to get addicted."

"You need to talk to Dr. Ness about it next week."

Later, during a lull in our whirlwind, I asked John, "Honey, do you understand you don't need to worry about getting addicted?" Briefly, I saw the question in his eyes, and then he grasped the meaning of my words.

The 8th was one of those bad news days. My sister-in-law called to tell me my brother, Bob, died. John's cough had loosened so much he was almost choking on what he coughed up. And then a phone call from Dr. Ness informed us he could not find any more funding for coverage of John's medicines. Yet we smiled, loved on each other, and rested in the peace that passes understanding.

At our next visit with Dr. Ness, John brought up the topic of air hunger and Dr. Markle's suggestion of taking Morphine. Before addressing that topic, Dr. Ness explained where John was in his journey. "I've ordered more bloodwork to be done. You can go by there on your way home. Your kidneys are stable for now. Normally, surgery would be performed on your hernia, but you are just not up to it. I suggest you wear a hernia belt. I will give you a prescription for Morphine. We need to discuss what Hospice can provide. They have two different focuses. If you are looking for relief, that is called palliative care. They will help you be comfortable while still taking drugs to prolong life and remain under doctor's care. If you are through with chemo and are exhausted with all the doctors, when you sign Hospice papers, there is a place to mark that you wish to no longer take life-prolonging drugs and will cease going to doctors. Then they will just help you be comfortable as you approach death. Morphine would be available to help you breathe. John, that decision is totally up to you. Just let me know."

I felt my insides flinch. *Have we reached that decision point already?* Apparently, we had. We held hands as we left his office. John knew I would support him either way, but it was looking like he would have to choose soon.

The next day we received a three-page statement from the lab where John's bloodwork had been sent. Several of the tests Dr. Ness requested had been deemed unnecessary. *What is wrong with people? He is fighting for his life. How do those in charge sleep at night? Do they just arbitrarily make rules that affect someone's life?*

It was time to have another visit with Dr. Arif at noon the next day. He prescribed an extra diuretic for John and explained that John's kidney function was down to 28%, but he felt the rest of the medical decisions needed to be made by Dr. Ness. By 12:45 we were headed back to Dr. Ness.

Dr. Ness walked us through the results of the blood test. "You are on fluid overload, called edema. You are also anemic. We need to work on your breathing first, then your kidneys. I'm prescribing some new medicine. We need to keep track of your blood pressure. Don't salt anything. Dr. Arif will be in touch with me. John, we will be working together to help you. Come back in two weeks."

Each evening, before bedtime (which occurred sometimes in a bed and other times in a recliner), our routine was to read from one of our favorite devotional books. We would sit side by side in the loveseat and take turns reading aloud the thought for that day. But John's breathing had become so difficult he could no longer take his turn. We held hands as I read, many times with my eyes leaking. Those moments were so precious; just the three of us, Jesus, John, and Joy, the three "Js" as John called us.

CHAPTER TWENTY-SEVEN

Weeks before, John had seen an announcement that Ernie Haase and Signature Sound were going to give a concert in Spokane, along with a group we had never heard called the Booth Brothers. John contacted our good friends Moe and Sandi in Spokane and arranged for us to drive up, attend the performance and then spend the night with them. As the time drew closer, his health had declined so quickly we discussed whether we should still make the trip. His desire to go overrode the weakness in his body, so plans were set in motion.

A few days before the concert, Sandi called to find out what John wanted to eat. Even though I tried to explain food was no longer that important to him, she had not been around to see his weakened condition. She prepared a delicious meal, but after only a few bites, I helped John to the bedroom so he could rest up for the evening. Moe helped me get him in the car and then drove right to the front door of the venue. We found a place to sit and wait while Moe parked and returned to help us. John wanted to sit in the front row, so that's what we did.

It was an excellent concert and he thoroughly enjoyed it. My attention was split between the singers and my frail husband beside me. One song by the Booth Brothers spoke to him particularly as a gift for Lorri. He waited while I made my way through the crowd to purchase the CD. Moe had gone to get the car and drove to the front door to pick us up. Exhausted, John went straight to bed, and we returned home the next day. Only later did Sandi and I have a chance to talk about his rapidly deteriorating condition.

The effort took its toll. He slept sporadically through the next day and night. Early in the morning, as I sat beside him, he said, "I feel like I'm dying." I thought, *he may be*. But that's not what I said. We spoke of our love for each other and how God was right there with us, covering us with His peace. I ended the brief talk with our customary declaration.

"I love you."

"More."

Three days later he was admitted to Trios Hospital with significant threat to life and function, words on the admittance form. I told the nurse, "He needs some form of nutrition, since he has just been laying there, not eating or drinking."

"We'll address that later."

Hooked to IVs, John remained motionless. A kidney test showed them functioning at 20%. It was Dr. Arif's day off, so his associate came by to check on him. That evening, John roused enough to eat a small bowl of chicken noodle soup, the first food since Spokane. Whatever was in the IV seemed to be working.

The next day, Dr. Ness came by and seemed pleased with John's response. "I've put you on Heparin to prevent blood clots and MiraLax for constipation, plus a pill to increase your appetite. We'll be watching your blood pressure since it's too low."

John desired one last trip to the ocean so he asked Dr. Ness if that could happen. "Let's give it a few days and see how you are doing. If possible, I want you to be able to go."

John was sleeping better even with all the endless interruptions, and his color was improving. Over the days of his hospitalization, friends (forty-one of them) took the time to come to his bedside. Some sat with him and allowed me to have a break (including bringing me a chai from Starbucks). What a varied group; church folk, motorcycle riders, neighbors, Starbucks gang and employees.

A text from a friend:

"Are you still doing okay? When might you get to go home?"

I responded: "He's sleeping but doing okay. Maybe tomorrow."

Two days later, a text from Trigg:

"Are you still in the hospital?"

"Yes, for now."

"Hopeful to go home tonight?"

"Yep."

"Okay. I'll check tomorrow."

He was discharged at 6:00 p.m.

The next day he received a text from his brother:

"How are you? Are you home?"

"Yes. I'm out of the hospital! I have multiple doctor appointments today and will probably be home early afternoon. Can we talk then? I'm just a little tired and sleep more than I used to."

Our first appointment of the day was with Dr. Ness. "I'm going to be looking into different chemo drugs – Nexavar and Sorafenib. I think you should go ahead and take your planned trip to the coast."

We drove to Dr. Arif's office. "Your blood pressure is too low so I'm taking you off one of your pills. You need to watch your weight and for leg swelling. If your weight keeps on increasing, you need to call me. Boss, I've given you a new prescription to increase your appetite. You need to do better about eating."

Just a side note: His weight gain had nothing to do with calories. It was water. Thus, he was still being urged to eat even as his weight increased.

John longed for one last trip to the ocean. Lorri had arranged for us to have a condo in Oregon, a place called Gleneden. With John's condition, that meant I would be doing the driving. Normally, a road trip is a delight for me. But he wanted me to drive the Cadillac, stating it would be much more comfortable for him than my car. My stress level spiked. I was uneasy behind the wheel of the larger car, and I would be going through unfamiliar towns. My love for him was the only reason I agreed. Between having to drive and my attention to his condition, the trip was not an enjoyable one for me. But he was able to lay the seat down and slept all the way.

Paul and Renee Null met us when we arrived and Paul helped me get John from the car to the condo, where he dozed in a recliner. We relished the time spent with very good friends as we talked of God's love and care for us. John never made it to the beach but enjoyed the view and sounds through an open window.

While we were there, we received a call from Dr. Ness. The chemo drug he prescribed had been approved by our insurance.

I was greatly relieved when we arrived home and the trip was behind me.

The next morning, we were in Dr. Arif's office. He had ordered a kidney function blood test, but it was not approved. "Boss, we'll just keep doing what we're doing. I'll be in touch with Dr. Ness."

The 4th of March found us in Dr. Ness's office. He had received the results from some of the tests run while John was in the hospital. "Your diagnosis is malignant neoplasm, an abnormal mass of tissue, with peripheral T-cells. According to your bloodwork, you are anemic and we may need to schedule a blood transfusion. You've lost ten pounds since the 23rd of February."

I asked about the side effects of enduring more chemo, since he was already so weak, tired and no appetite. "How can he get worse?"

"It's up to John if he wants to continue."

A one-word answer came from John. "No."

I asked, "What is making him feel this way? Is it the cancer? Meds?"

"Cancer."

Another question: "What happens if he takes Morphine pills around the clock, more often than every eight hours?"

"Go to every six hours. And for nourishment he needs to drink Ensure, Boost, Carnation Breakfast or Lucerna."

We traveled from there to the office of Dr. Arif. Once again, we heard that John had lost ten pounds and needed to do better with his nourishment. "Make a smoothie. Drink shakes. Your blood sugar is not too high for now and your kidney function is up slightly to 30%. I've ordered some more bloodwork. Call for an appointment any time you feel you need to."

John said, "I feel like I'm fading fast."

"Boss, we are doing what we can. Isn't there anything that sounds good to eat?"

"Yes. Strawberry milkshakes. But I can't have those."

"Why not? Sounds like something that would work."

"I'm diabetic."

There was a pause and then Dr. Arif said, "Boss." It took John a moment before the message was received. He could eat whatever he wanted. Diabetes was not going to be the cause of his demise.

When the word got out that John was drinking strawberry milkshakes, they began to magically appear. Friends brought one to our door on a regular basis, and sometimes we had two or three backups in the freezer. They didn't taste like cardboard and his delight was evident. Did my heart good to see him enjoying them.

That evening, seated side by side on the loveseat, John shared with me, "Joy, I'm through. I've done everything all the doctors have asked of me. I'm tired. I'm ready. Let's just pray it's the kidney cancer that takes me and not the lung cancer. Sounds like a much easier way to go. You have been my rock and I know you are exhausted too. I have never loved you more. My remaining days belong to God."

I didn't like it, but I understood.

CHAPTER TWENTY-EIGHT

March 5th began with a visit to Dr. Markle. "I'm giving you a prescription for an anti-depressant which will help lift the fog you're experiencing because the receptors in your brain have been altered. The first week on the medicine is worst for side effects. If you go with Hospice, they can call me regarding it. Anti-anxiety meds can be used in conjunction with Morphine."

"What is the process to get a handicap tag for our car?' John had struggled to acquiesce to the reality he needed that card hanging from our rearview mirror, but he no longer had the strength to walk very far. This question was a sign of his acceptance.

When John's concerns had been addressed, we drove to the Washington State Department of Licensing to apply for the Disabled Parking Placard. Dr. Markle had filled out his section, indicating it would be a temporary authorization. No fee was required and one more step had been taken in John's dwindling life journey. I was in awe of his attitude, as he surmounted each phase with poise.

That afternoon he received a text from Trigg:

"Just thought I would let you know I want to be included with the involvement of Hospice."

John: "Tears."

Trigg: "Me too."

An appointment was made with Hospice to come to our home for an assessment the next day. I felt like I was on the periphery of a drama evolving before my eyes. How could it be real? Hospice?

At 10:00 am, a nurse arrived with brochures and questions. I needed some answers myself and asked, "What do I do when he falls?"

"You have to call Hospice first before you call 911. Put the number on the front of the refrigerator. If you don't call Hospice first, you will be removed from the program."

"How quickly will that be? What if he's bleeding?"

"You just need to call Hospice."

I wasn't feeling reassured.

She continued. "Hospice has a contract with Medicare, but we will still be in charge of what happens. After having so many doctors, you will now have only one, Dr. Kohan. If you feel you need the doctor, call the Hospice number. A nurse will be available around the clock to answer questions. We will do nothing to address the cancer. A team will come out and explain all these details."

After more discussion and many questions, she asked, "Are you ready to sign the form?"

She placed a lime green form on the table in front of John. In Part A he checked the box beside: DNAR/Do Not Attempt Resuscitation (Allow Natural Death). Part B he had three choices: Comfort Measures Only, Limited Additional Interventions or Full Treatment. He checked the box for Comfort Measures Only/Patient prefers no hospital transfer. I felt my heart shatter into a million pieces as I watched my beloved sign his name and date it. That form was then displayed on the kitchen cupboard, accessible to any emergency personnel who might come to our house. Once we had it taped in place, we wrapped our arms around each other and just stood silently, connecting deeply. Each step on this path drew us closer.

Three days later, a nurse, social worker and chaplain arrived to clarify what to expect. "Someone will come out once a week, but you can reach a nurse by phone from 8:00 to 5:00. As his condition deteriorates, they will come more often."

I asked. "We were told a nurse would be available around the clock. Now you are saying 8:00 to 5:00. Which one is right?"

"We have a person answering the phone around the clock. If they decide you need to talk to a nurse, they can contact one for you." Then she listened to his lungs and left.

Dr. Ness called to say he received a letter regarding his appeal that John's chest x-rays be covered. They were denied as they did not deem them a medical necessity. I no longer reacted to the callousness of those making decisions about our journey. Their rejection was just par for the course.

A Hospice nurse stopped by on the 18th. I helped John to the table so we could talk. Her advice, add more spice and herbs to his food to see if it tastes better. That was the extent of that stopover.

Later that day, Pastor Phil came by for a visit and they spent an uplifting time together. I was so grateful for such wonderful friends supporting us.

An email from Paul Null brought back many memories.

"Here's to five years of happy memories. I am so very blessed to have been able to share some of them as a guest in your home. I recall Matthew parties and birthday parties and small group get-togethers, not to mention Sunday afternoon lunches. But what stands out the most is the times late in the evening after Relational Elder Training when the three of us would sit down over coffee and sweet treats and talk about our journey with the Lord.

A deep and abiding friendship has grown out of those times, and I will never forget that it was born out of your gracious hospitality to welcome me as a guest every other week for that wonderful year. I am honored to call you Brother and Sister in Christ. You have given me a taste of heaven in your home.

Lots of love in Him."

Soon it was time to celebrate the fifth anniversary of when we moved into our wonderful home. But this year I wanted it to be more than just our regular party. It would also be a time to say goodbye. The invitation I sent out requested that each guest write a card or letter to John for me to read to him later. A basket to collect them was placed on the table in the front hall. John lay in the recliner in the living room as seventy friends gathered, taking turns to sit by him and visit. The decibel level grew as talk and laughter filled the rooms. A bittersweet evening.

After he went to bed, I sat on the edge beside him with the basket in my lap. Tears filled our eyes as we were inundated with love and caring from the words written. Several times I had to pause in my reading to gain control of my emotions. We were wrapped in such tenderness from these folks we loved.

The basket contained one item that was not a card, but a pair of bicycle shorts. As I held them up for John to see, laughter mingled with tears and we recalled an incident years before. We had gone to Starbucks on a Saturday morning. One of the young women in our group had on her bicycle riding clothes for a ride later. She was sitting next to John, and I noticed him repeatedly glancing downward at what seemed to be her legs. In front of everyone, I asked, "John, what are you doing?" "I'm just trying to read her shorts." The group erupted in laughter. The words around the cuff were in a different language. When I pulled those shorts from the basket, we received the message loud and clear.

Spring Break arrived for our teacher daughter, Lorri. She flew from Georgia to Portland, where I picked her up. She was totally unaware of the huge surprise in store for her. John was like a little kid at Christmas and wanted to tell her the minute we walked into the house. But he managed to restrain himself until the proper moment. Two days later, as the three of us visited in the family room, John looked at me and asked, "Is it time?" I nodded. (Just a side note: I married John when Lorri was 14.)

"Lorri, you asked me to write you a letter before I go. I've tried my best to come up with words to say about how I feel, and I haven't been able to do it. I think actions speak louder than words. What if I adopt you?"

Lorri jumped up from the couch and hurried to throw her arms around him. There were no dry eyes. Our lawyer friend had made special arrangements for Lorri to be adopted while she was here, but we had to wait another three days for that momentous occasion.

Hospice ordered a wheelchair for John, and it was delivered later that day. I tried to absorb the fact that my motorcycle riding beloved was so frail he could no longer walk safely without falling.

John began each morning asking what time it was, so I purchased a clock with large red numbers and placed it where he could see it from the bed. Many days, he asked, "Have you heard from Dean? Do you think he's going to come see me?" Oh, how that hurt my heart. I could not be Dean to him, and he never came. Until John's illness, Dean had been one of his best friends.

We had been on a doctor merry-go-round for so many months, the cessation of doctor visits created a sensation of falling off a cliff. John and I would start to talk about the next appointment with a certain doctor and then remember there was no next appointment. We missed our connections to Dr. Markle, Dr. Ness and Dr. Arif. Even though Hospice had a doctor's name on their printed forms, we never saw him.

The highlight of John's day was 3:00 pm when his Starbucks friends met at our table instead of at Starbucks. Lorri provided cookies and we had a Keurig with several kinds of coffee. The front door was unlocked; they came in and made themselves at home. Those friends gave John something I could not, a feeling of belonging to a gathering where he was included as an equal, not someone dying.

CHAPTER TWENTY-NINE

Adoption Day arrived, March 26th. Excitement filled our home as we dressed for the occasion. With the wheelchair loaded in the back, we helped John to the car. When we arrived at the Justice Center, I walked behind Lorri and John and watched as she proudly pushed him in the wheelchair. The love between them was palpable. Tyson met us there, camera in hand. Even though pictures were not normally allowed inside the courtroom, we had been given special permission since this was a rather rare occurrence.

Our lawyer friend had already arrived and stood in front of the magistrate ready to say the proper words to make this official. Then it was the judge's turn to do his duty, following the prescribed protocol. After the questions had been asked and answered, the adoption of Lorri by John was finalized. She was now a Bach. Tears rolled freely down our faces. The judge came down from his bench to congratulate the new father/daughter. With a grin, he added, "We usually give a stuffed animal to the child when they are adopted. Would you like one?" Lorri laughed and picked out a bear from the proffered tray, which she promptly named Bach Bear. When we were through, she pushed John back to the car, with Bach Bear in his lap.

Lorri asked John if she could post about her special day on Facebook, including a photo of the two of them. His request was, "Just don't let the wheelchair show." It received fifty-nine comments of tenderness and congratulations.

All too soon, it was time for her to return to Georgia. Realizing this might be their final goodbye, it was extremely difficult for her to leave.

I kept thinking my heart couldn't take any more. *Oh God, please help us all make it through this. Give Lorri peace as she boards that plane. We place our pain in your compassionate hands.*

Love and help came from every direction. Our church sent out a call to do some needed yard work and a group showed up. We received beautiful flower arrangements, which certainly brightened the inside of our home. And I'll not forget the food. Our neighbor would make him some soup, call me and say, "I've made John some soup. Bring a pan to the fence and I'll empty my pan into yours." Several varieties of soup filled our refrigerator, dropped off by caring friends. Since all food seemed to have no taste (or a bad taste), he went through stages of binging on the one that worked. French Onion soup became one of his favorites, which arrived at our front door every week. One neighbor supplied dessert and Lorri provided an assortment of cookies from her Bachery, so we could offer refreshments to our visitors. Folks didn't forget me. I had no time or energy to think of food, but I ate very well.

When we built our house, we had a say in everything. John was very specific about his office. It had a large window to enable him to see the fireplace in the living room and the fire pit on the patio. The cupboards, the countertop around two walls, the lighting; he designed it all. One night his voice woke me with a question.

"Joy, what are you going to do with my office?"

"John, it's the middle of the night."

"I've been laying here awake for hours wondering. I designed it specifically for me, so what will you do with it?"

"I'm going to paint it pink. Now go to sleep."

"I'm serious. What do you think you will use it for?"

"I haven't even thought about it, so give me some time. Can we talk about it sometime during the day?"

"Okay, I'll give you a few days."

Later I told him I would turn it into my financial office where I paid the bills, etc. Also, I would use it for my Bible study room. He was satisfied.

The Starbucks gang continued their fellowship with John each day. Tyson sometimes joined in, and he had observed how difficult it was for John to rise from the dining room chair, unable to do so without help. So, he brought a bar stool from his home for John to use. What a relief for John to just be able to slide to a standing position.

The 14th of April, their time together was over, and they headed to their cars. As I walked them to the door, John tried to move from the dining room table to the big chair in the TV room by himself. I had stepped outside when I heard him yell my name and I hurried to see what was wrong. He lay on the floor with a bloody face. He had tumbled headfirst into the bookshelf. Running back to the door, I yelled at the last two friends getting in their cars. "John has fallen, and I need your help." Gene and I helped him up and navigated him to the chair. Victoria washed the blood from his face and cleaned the stains on the carpet. Humbled, he profusely thanked them. It was just another demonstration of their obvious affection and compassion. His face bore the evidence of that mishap for several days.

A Hospice nurse came by the next day and had many questions about what happened to cause John's fall. "Next time I come, I will bring a cane and a baby monitor."

Text from a friend to John:

"Joy says no joking about your fall. I say just tell them you got new feet and haven't figured out how to use them yet."

"Just trying to look like a tough guy."

"You are tougher than the rest of us."

Over the previous weeks we had occasionally discussed what funeral home to use. After choosing one, John placed a phone call and was told someone would get back to him. Never happened. So, he called another one and spoke with a very cordial lady who took down his information and scheduled a time for a home visit, since John was so weak. A nicely dressed man arrived and we settled at the dining room table. He took brochures from his briefcase and began discussing various styles and prices of coffins.

John said, "I wish to be cremated, so there will be no coffin. Do you cremate?"

It was then I noticed the man's name on his jacket. Blaze. As he explained they did cremation, I began laughing. Of course, I received strange looks from both men.

"Sorry. Couldn't help it. With a name like Blaze, I find it very appropriate you cremate." More laughter.

Blaze brought out more brochures displaying urns. Large ones. Big enough for all the ashes. John looked at me and asked, "Are you going to set me on the mantel?"

"You're not setting on my mantel."

"I think I know what you'll do with me. Does it involve a mountain?"

"Yes. The motorcycle gang will take you to the top of Dooley Mountain and have a little ceremony."

During this conversation, I had observed the varied expressions on Blaze's face. I imagine he had never witnessed that kind of discussion before. John loved those twisties and was very pleased with the arrangements. It was important to me that John be honored for fulfilling his military duty. But the authorization for that depended on finding his Honorable Discharge papers. Blaze explained the secretary at the funeral home could help me locate them. "You can request to be given the shells from the gun salute. We have a company that will put some of John's ashes in them and then seal them. We can also create the brochure for the funeral."

John corrected him. "I'm not having a funeral. It will be a graduation party at my church, complete with balloons."

Once again, Blaze took it all in stride.

A week later, the nurse from Hospice came by. No cane. No baby monitor. After checking his vital signs, she looked at me and said, "He seems depressed. You need to take him on a vacation." What was she thinking? I could barely get him from room to room in the house. He slept most of the time. Neither of us would enjoy a vacation. After she left, I called Hospice, described what had been recommended and asked for a different nurse.

A walker had now been provided by Hospice. I surveyed the whole house for anything on the floor that could possibly contribute to a fall. All the throw rugs had been removed. John struggled to get the hang of using it. Just going from the bed to the bathroom became challenging. I felt my heart in my throat as he tipped and slid his way there and back.

Then came the middle of the night when the tumble came. I was walking beside him, but knew if he headed down, I could not suspend the fall. He uttered a moan as his body began to tilt. As if in slow motion, he crumpled to the left and landed on the tile floor.

I knelt beside him. "John, are you okay? Babe, talk to me. I need to know if you are okay." He said not a word; just stared into the distance. I grabbed towels from the shelf and placed them under his head, ran from the room to get a cover for him. Still silence from the floor. Following instructions not to call 911, I called the Hospice number and got an answering service.

"My husband has just fallen on the tile floor, and I need help to get him up."

That statement was followed by questions...his name...date of birth, etc. Absolutely no hurry on their part. "What is your phone number? I'll have someone call you."

Fifteen minutes later I received a call from a nurse. "I was told you needed to talk to me." I repeated my story. I heard clicking on a keyboard. She began asking questions that had no connection to us. I interrupted her. "I believe you are looking at the wrong patient." I then repeated our information. Thirty minutes later, she agreed to call someone to come out. Within three minutes paramedics were at my door.

Such nice young men. Gently they carried him to the bed. John still had not spoken. I escorted the paramedics toward the door. One turned and asked, "Is there anything else we can do for you?"

"Yes, tell him to stop trying to get out of bed. I can't get him up when he falls." They turned and walked back to the bedroom. I have no idea what was said, but he never tried walking to the bathroom again.

Every week, a few women gathered at our home for prayer time, such a bright spot in my day. Originally, the dining room table had been our meeting place. As John's condition worsened, he moved to the bed more regularly. Since the table was right outside the bedroom door, we relocated to another room. When the baby monitor was finally provided, we adjusted to the sounds emitted from it and became instantly aware if he was in need.

When John became dependent on insulin, he had taken charge of administering it. It was a lot of work to test his blood sugar, calculate how much insulin he would need, fill the syringe with the correct amount and then give the shot in his abdomen. One evening, sitting on the side of the bed, he asked me to bring the paraphernalia to him.

He guided me through how to fill the syringe and I handed it to him. His hand shook as he reached for it.

"Honey, I don't know if I figured it right. I can't think straight anymore. I'm too shaky to administer it. You are going to have to give me the shot." Inwardly I began to panic. I had never given a shot before. As I bent to follow his directions, he took my hand in his. "I'm through doing this. I'm in the last stages of dying. Why am I putting us through this? Please take it all back and put it away."

When this journey began, we had agreed that he was in charge of what happened to him medically. If he was done with insulin, then he was through. I placed the insulin pack back in the refrigerator. It was never used again.

CHAPTER THIRTY

When our neighbor, Dan, bought a pontoon boat, John and I had been invited to join him and his wife on a float down the Columbia River, which John thoroughly enjoyed. As his world grew smaller, he talked about memories outside our home, including that trip. So, I reached out to Dan and asked if another float could be arranged, explaining how weak John had become. Dan was delighted to be able to fulfill a wish for John. We decided Tyson would be a good person to assist him in pulling it off.

When Tyson called to tell John the plan, I could see the excitement on John's face. He wanted to go right now, but he had to wait until the next day. Dan and Tyson helped John from the bedroom to the front door, where I said, "Have a great time, honey," and closed the door. It would be a few hours respite for me.

Days later I heard the rest of the story. The reason I know what happened is because the Starbucks gang was seated around our table when John said, "I inspected the sprinkler system the other day." Standing in the kitchen, I paused to hear the rest of that story. "My friends helped me to the yard and then let go of me to get the car door open. When they turned back around, I was face down in the yard. Scared them to death. I wasn't hurt, but they felt so bad that they had failed to take care of me. I never told Joy it happened."

"And now you have," I said from behind his chair. Laughter erupted around the table.

But there was more to that story. That evening, John said, "Babe, thanks so much for arranging that float down the river. You know I loved it. I wanted my picture taken, so Tyson got his camera ready. But I said I wanted to be standing up when he took it. They both argued with me. I won." Now that I knew the whole tale, he produced a photo for me to see. There stood my weak husband, no life jacket, proudly floating down the middle of the river.

The 5th of May brought a visitor with gifts, several little brown paper sacks. Before he left Idaho, Sky, the new lab owner, had purchased a variety of edible hemp for John. Our knowledge of edible hemp was zero, so he explained the different choices available.

"Sky, thanks so much for thinking of me, but I'm past eating."

"Well, I'll leave them here in case you change your mind."

After he left, a row of little brown bags sat on the counter in the laundry room. My mind always did a double take when I saw them. Edible hemp! Who knew I would have a supply of that?

A week later I welcomed a small group of musicians from our church into the bedroom, intending to give him a little concert. They sang for an hour and then Michael, our music director, asked him, "So, did you enjoy that?" Inwardly I cringed. Apparently, Michael was unaware that John did not care for his style of music and would stay in the foyer of the church until the music portion of the service was over. *What will John say?*

I didn't have to wait long.

"I'm dying and cannot tell a lie. No, I did not."

A moment of silence and then laughter. All was well.

Our small group continued to gather at our home every week, but I had assumed the leadership. As John became weaker, he stayed as long as he could and then would ask for help to get to bed. After he was settled, we continued with our study. By now the baby monitor had become a constant in my life, and as a group we stayed attuned to his needs.

When the nurse from Hospice came, I shared with her the book I had discovered online called *Final Gifts* to help me know about the process of dying. She seemed surprised and told me, "Oh, I have that book and could have given you a copy." Too late. I already bought it.

She continued, "I'm going to order a hospital bed and recliner chair for him. And I see he's taking some meds he should have discontinued when Hospice took over. We are just now realizing that."

That same day, Tyson met with the Realtor who would be selling our lab building. As a builder, Tyson knew all the right questions to ask, which I did not. John was incapable of handling any more business transactions.

When the Starbucks gang came that afternoon, as usual they asked if there was anything they could do to help. My answer was "yes". I requested they dismantle our bed and haul it to the garage in preparation for the delivery of a hospital bed the next day. John and I slept in the TV room that night. The next morning a fully electric bed with mattress, bed rails and a trapeze bar to hang above him was provided. Side note: The promised recliner never arrived.

What ensued was an unusual comedy routine. John still wanted me to lay beside him. My husband's life was ebbing away, and we hungered to be close. But there were reasons why that couldn't happen. Have you seen how narrow those beds are? Plus, he needed the head to be raised to ease his struggle to breathe. Good thing no one had a video camera. It just might have looked a little weird as we tried various positions. We had to accept the fact it wasn't going to work. My solution to that problem was to rent a second hospital bed for me and place it next to his.

The second bed was delivered and right away I saw there were still issues. If I laid with my head at the top end of my bed, all I could see was the back of the raised section of his bed. Our desire for closeness would not be met. Within minutes of laying down, I was up again, rearranging my bed so my head was next to the foot of his bed. If I laid on my side, I could see his precious face. I placed my pillow on his bed, beside his feet and my hand gripped his ankle. That achieved our yearning for physical touch. His eyes would be shut, but he could tell I was still there.

The Cadillac John had purchased at Christmas time now sat in the garage undriven. Even though the Archibald's dealership didn't usually sell someone's car for them, they offered to help me. We had known them for years and between our personal lives and our business, we had purchased several cars (and one motorcycle) from their car lot. I threw in the regular muffler too just in case the new owner preferred a quiet ride instead of the very noisy Borla muffler John had installed. Archibald's promised they would make sure it got a good home. It didn't take very many days before it was sold to a man who displayed the very same kind of grin that had been on John's face. And even though John had purchased the Cadillac from the car dealer next door to them, they also helped me navigate the process of asking for a refund on the two-year warranty John had taken out five months previously.

The loss of the Cadillac affected me more than it did John. He had watched his motorcycles go down the street when he sold them. John's world now consisted of the bedroom, so he really didn't miss that the Cadillac was no longer in the garage. Our modes of transportation had dwindled from two motorcycles and two cars to one car. The garage seemed empty.

Frequently John would say to me, "I know you're going to be okay." I would agree but didn't understand why he repeatedly said that. *Does he really think I am just going to breeze through this?* One day I finally asked, "Why do you keep saying that to me. I love you with all my heart and will miss you terribly." His response, "Because I'm leaving you and I need to know you'll be okay." He just needed reassurance, which I gladly gave him.

Friends continued to text and email him, some asking if they could come by. Many times, I was the one to respond since he was asleep. "This is Joy. He sleeps all the time. Just drop by and we'll wake him up. He would be delighted to see you."

Some people were a little bit more difficult to deal with. They had decided John needed to eat, so would arrive with something special they had made just for him. He would thank them, but say he wasn't hungry. One lady would not take no for an answer. She looked at me and said, "Joy, you need to make him eat. You are supposed to be taking care of him." I had read the book that said the dying person knows when it's time to stop eating. I asked her to come out of the bedroom with me and then tried to explain he was in charge of this journey, and he was through eating. She thought that was a bunch of nonsense and said so.

John's battle to breathe became more and more labored and noisy, the sound filling the house. *How can I live with that constant reminder that his breath is deteriorating? God, I need you to help block that sound from my consciousness. There is no way I can escape it.* I can't say I no longer heard it, but the overpowering sense of anguish was reduced. One day while I was standing in the kitchen talking on the phone to Lorri she asked, "What is that awful noise I hear?"

"That is John struggling to breathe." We cried together.

We had known Sky's dad, Bob, for years. The next time Sky came to town, he texted John, "Bob is with me. Do you want me to swing him by before I go the lab? You can have a nice long visit." John's phone was now in my possession, so I responded, "This is Joy. I'll get him ready."

I placed a chair for Bob beside John's bed, brought them some water and asked if there was anything else I needed to do. I was not expecting John's response. He pointed to the open door behind me, which led to the bathroom. "Get them out of there." I looked and saw no one. "Honey, there's no one in there." "Yes, there is, and they need to leave now." Uncertain what to do, I stood looking at John, who said, "I need to have an important talk with Bob. They don't want me to. Make them leave."

I turned, walked to the bathroom door and said, "In the name of Jesus, I command you to leave." Then I moved to John's bedside and asked, "Are they gone?" "Yes, thank you."

The serious discussion took place. After Bob left, John shared with me he had spoken of God and His love, of His caring for Bob, and of his need to have a relationship with Jesus. In their time of conversation, Bob accepted Jesus into his heart. His mission complete, John slept in peace.

When Bob and Sky went home, the little brown bags went with them.

CHAPTER THIRTY-ONE

For years, part of our daily routine had been to say, "I love you" to each other. The typical response was, "More". But as May passed, John's response changed. When I told him I loved him, he would say, "I know". I felt this was a signal he knew the end was drawing near. Inwardly, I braced myself for the inevitable.

When Hospice came the next time, it was a nurse and a social worker. John was no longer able to come to the table, so I was asked questions about how he was doing.

"He feels like he needs to go to the bathroom every hour or two. He can no longer make it in there, so can I have some Depends to put on him, so he won't try to get up? The nights are the worst. When he falls, I need help getting him up from the floor and you have said I can't call 911. One time it took me 45 minutes to get him back on the bed and I pulled something in my back."

"Here is a number you can call for lift assistance. Medicare changed their criteria for end of life, and here is the new information," she said as she handed me a brochure. "We will start the process for a bath aid who will come in the next few days."

When I could, I began making arrangement for John's service. We had discussed it and he had put in writing what he did and did not want. It was to be a graduation party, complete with balloons. He also made it plain what he wanted the brochure to say. "Everyone knows I'm not perfect. How about Celebrating the Life of an Imperfect Man?"

The party supplies I had ordered began arriving. The Mylar balloons said "Congratulations!" and "Way to go, graduate!". A friend arranged to provide helium for them. Another friend offered to do the decorating at the church. I felt very conflicted working with festive decorations while my husband lay dying in the other room, even though I was aware he would never see them. With tears in my eyes, I called the funeral home and asked them to set aside a shadow box for the folded flag. Already I was deep into the grieving process. The ever-present baby monitor was at my side while I worked.

John became irrational and agitated. Over the days, he said some things that didn't make sense.

"I want to get a newspaper."

"What are you looking for?"

"I want a newspaper for you so you can read it."

As his hands fluttered over the covers, I asked, "What are you doing?"

"Folding clothes."

He continued with his random statements. "Are you ready to download yet?"

"Did you hear about Mom?"

"What about Mom?"

"Is she home?"

"Is she?"

"I don't know."

His mom died when he was a teenager.

"You can leave the bedroom door open."

"For me to live is Christ and to die is gain."

He told Trigg about the night he lay on the bathroom floor so long before Hospice finally let me call someone. "That was a test. He didn't come."

"I need you to come into the office."

"What are we going in there for?"

"So you can take some dictation."

He kept repeating the word dictation. It seemed very important. I found a notepad and pen and sat by the bed. "Okay, John, I'm ready. What do you want me to write?"

He began saying names, six in all. I wrote as he talked. I knew the first five, but when he told me the sixth one it was new to me. *Rocky. Who was Rocky? And what were these names?*

He asked me to call his brother and hold the phone to his ear so he could tell him goodbye.

John's hospital bed had come complete with a grab bar above his head, a metal triangle he could use to pull himself up in the bed if he slid down the raised section. The triangle was held to the frame with a chain. That chain became an issue.

Night and day no longer had any meaning to him; it was all the same. The business of dying keeps different hours than the business of living. When not asleep, he became bored. Then he discovered the grab bar. More explicitly, the chain holding the bar. If he batted his hand back and forth on the bar, the chain rattled…LOUDLY. He enjoyed that. In the middle of the night, it was a rude awakening for me. I learned if I saw his hand sneaking upward, rattling was on the way.

"Why do you do that?"

"I like the sound."

I had no argument. He was dying and if he enjoyed rattling the chain, who was I to ask him to stop.

My emotions were stuffed so far inside, I wondered if I could ever feel again. But I had a job to do, be there for him. He mentioned many times how he appreciated the way I was coping with his dying. "It makes it so much easier for me that you aren't crying all the time." That was my goal, to make his journey as stress-free as possible.

God was my constant companion. I now understood the scripture about pray without ceasing. I sent prayers heavenward every waking moment. He slept most of the time, but my alert button never turned off. The light on the dresser remained on all night. When I laid down, I kept my glasses on so I could immediately see what his need might be.

His wallet and money from his pants pocket now lay on the kitchen counter where he placed them several weeks ago. His special sunglasses that made him feel so cool as he drove his red Cadillac were close by. He has no need for them.

Our garage was designed to hold two motorcycles, his car and mine. One solitary car remains. Even the handicap placard that allowed him to park closer to buildings has joined the unused symbols of a busy life. He has no need for them.

The double towel holder that was installed when we built this house now holds a lonely towel. I will never need two. And he is far too weak to take a shower, so his towel has been washed, dried and folded. He has no need for it.

His clothes and shoes in the closet are just as he left them the last time he wore clothes. He has no need for them.

This is what it's like at the end of a life. All the accoutrements we consider so important no longer have any value. He is going on a journey without me. Even though I can't accompany him, we both know Someone who can. We've placed our trust in Him.

A text from Lorri said, "Love you, Dad."

He responded: "Love you."

Even though she texted regularly, that was the last time he answered.

I shared with Tyson's wife, Linda, about the six names, puzzled as to what they were. She had been with me at the funeral home when it was explained to me that even though John was to be cremated, he could have six honorary pallbearers, and she reminded me of that. *Of course. The first five made sense, but who was Rocky?*

On May 22nd, a Hospice nurse came to give him a sponge bath, the first one provided by them. While she was there, she asked to speak to me before she left. After exiting the bedroom, she said, "He may have only a week or two left. When he passes, you are to call us immediately. You need to know he may be here for hours after his death. Arrangements will need to be made for someone to come out and pronounce him and then we will call the funeral home to come get his body."

I had been given a huge piece of information that my mind couldn't seem to compute. He would just lay here dead for hours. I felt like I was hanging on by a thread. And he wasn't just a body, he was my beloved. My heart hurt.

I had promised John he could die at home. He didn't want to be in some unknown room with strangers taking care of him. I understood, but I was wearing out and needed help. Riddled with guilt, I called the Hospice House. When we signed up, we had been told there was a respite room available for when I had reached my limit. John could be moved there for three days while I recouped.

"This is Joy Bach and I'm calling regarding my husband, John. I am his caretaker and was told that when I needed a break, he could be moved to the Hospice House for three days to give me a chance to rest.

I am calling to make those arrangements."

I heard fingers tapping on a keyboard and then a long pause.

"I'm looking at his records now and he does not qualify for that benefit."

"I thought the Hospice House was for those who are dying. He is dying."

"Yes, that's partially true. But the respite service is only for those who need help with pain management. His records show he is not in pain. I can give you a list of nurses available who can come to your house and take care of him. Their rate is $25 an hour."

I had no words. I couldn't afford that. Someone had given me false information that I had subconsciously counted on. Too numb for tears, I disconnected the call.

Over the weeks, my daughters had volunteered to come and help, but I thought I would need them more later, so I said no. They lived in other states and had jobs with a lot of responsibility. Besides, I was unsure how long these last days would take. I was in uncharted territory, uncertain of my next move. *I'm on my own.* And just that quickly, I knew I was not. Loving arms held me. My strength would come from God.

CHAPTER THIRTY-TWO

Tyson came by to check on how we were doing. He was such a dear friend who had worked so hard when building our house to make sure John had exactly the Jacuzzi tub he wanted, not knowing how very important that would become. When he realized I wasn't doing well, he immediately volunteered to stay with John for a while. I quickly wrote him some instructions before I left. "He has on Depends so does not need to get out of bed to go to the bathroom. He will fight you on this. He may want to sit on the side of the bed and use the urinal. We have tried this many times. Nothing ever happens. You may have to help him turn over. If he wants a drink, he needs help getting the straw in his mouth. The drink is on the nightstand. If he needs more, it is Propel and is in the door of the refrigerator. If he asks for a Boost, that is on the top shelf in the refrigerator. Plug the baby monitor in beside you if you leave the room so you can hear what's happening in the bedroom. If he asks about putting on shorts, they are on the dresser."

As I walked to my car, I thought about that note. It was like I was leaving a young child in the care of a babysitter. In many ways John had reverted to childhood, with basic needs to be met. I had to let go of what was happening in my house and give my mind a rest. I drove to a quiet place along the river, talked to God and stared at the water flowing past, releasing my concerns into the current. Hours later I was in a much better frame of mind and returned home. Tyson had made a note for me. "Three times he took some sips of water. He attempted to use the urinal without success. Bill and Carmen came by at 10:45 and left at 11:10."

Tyson and I sat at the table outside John's bedroom door and he said, "I think it's necessary for you to have someone else here all the time, especially a man. Let me go home and make some arrangements and then I'll be back to spend the night." Those words were a balm to my soul. He was correct. I wasn't strong enough to control John, especially when he tried to get out of bed. I did need a man and Tyson was stepping into that void.

Tyson was by my side in the middle of the night when John began throwing up and pooping. My heart overflowed with gratefulness as he helped me with the clean-up job. *John hasn't eaten for days and barely taken sips of water. How is there anything left to expel from his body?*

John continued to talk randomly.

"I didn't realize we moved. The environment here is so different."

"Tell everyone it's ready."

"What's ready?"

"Breakfast. Tell Tyson to come and eat."

John asked that I call Lorri and hold the phone to his ear. He struggled for breath as he said his last words to her. I thought my heart was already broken, but I discovered it could break some more as I heard him say, "Your word is daughter." She and I made it through the phone call, but as we talked later, we fell apart.

The sound of John's efforts to breathe filled the house, a sound I had been living with for days. *How can I ever get used to this horrible noise?*

I could tell he was trying to get everything taken care of before he left. He asked for one more phone call, this time to our pastor who was out of town at a meeting. Once more I felt my heart shattering into smaller pieces as he told Pastor Phil, "You aren't going to make it back in time, but that's okay. I'll see you again someday."

That evening I posted this to his Facebook page:

"I sure didn't expect this day to come." A quote this morning from John. He wanted to convey so much to you, his friends. But his mind just can't put the words together. He has been under hospice care for several weeks. I think he was trying to say "goodbye". Posted by his wife.

As I read the fifty-four comments written there, I could barely see through my tears. The deep love flowing from the words on that post soothed my soul.

May 23rd introduced a new and devastating recurring incidence. The look of utter terror in his eyes when he couldn't get his breath ripped my already splintered heart to smithereens. I will never forget the pleading in his eyes, begging me to help him. Tyson, Trigg and I stood at the foot of his bed and assessed the situation. I had been told the container given to me by Hospice to store in the refrigerator had liquid Morphine in it. We believed Morphine would relieve his desperate attempt to inhale oxygen. I broke the seal on the box, removed the Morphine and dropper and handed them to Tyson. Trigg and I held John still as Tyson placed a drop under his tongue. Within minutes, the restlessness had ceased and he slept.

May 24th – a text to me from Pastor Phil:

"How are you both doing today? You are in our prayers."

"He's struggling at the moment. Throwing up. Has a crackle in his throat. Saying I'm tired of being on this slow road. I want the highway."

Trigg came when she could and sat by him, with her small dog, Vivien, asleep on his bed. There wasn't room for our large labradoodle on there too, so Charlie laid at the edge of my bed next to John. He was unaware of their presence.

May 24th – 8:49 pm - a text to John from Sky:

"You up?"

I responded: "No, he's asleep. You need to use my phone number from now on. He's failing fast."

Outside, the nation was celebrating Memorial Day weekend. Inside, our days and nights blurred together as we kept vigil over John's emaciated body. Trigg was now staying with me too, so the three of us watched over his every need.

His breathing pattern changed. He would undergo periods of gasping and rapid breathing, followed by a time of silence. As I waited to see if he was ever going to breathe again, I steeled myself for the cessation of his life. Then the cycle would repeat. This ever-present reminder of his looming death was a constant drain on my already tattered emotions. I could feel God in the very atmosphere of the room, holding me together, whispering in my ear "My child, I am here."

Early the next morning, I received a text from Pastor Phil asking how we were doing.

"He was awake all night with stuff in his throat he can't cough up. Tyson is now staying with me, and he has taken Elder status to a whole new level. Earlier I was going to take a shower, but John said no, that he needed me here to guide him."

"Thanks for keeping us up to date. Is Hospice available to come help you through this time?"

"Pretty much no. I'm supposed to have friends help or hire someone."

"I'm so sorry. I wish we could be there for you. We will be home tomorrow night late.

Once again John's respiration pattern changed. I was so very in tune with every nuance of his breathing, I heard it immediately…and knew what it was….the death rattle. The book had warned about this possibility. It's a combination of gurgling and rattling noises, because he was no longer able to swallow or cough. Very unsettling to hear but didn't seem to bother him. Just one of the last signals that his life was ending.

Tuesday morning on the 26th, Tyson explained he needed to go to his work site and get his building crew started for the day. "But I've asked a friend to come and sit with John while I'm gone."

"Do I know him?"

"I don't think so, but his name is Rocky."

My mind did a little flip-flop. *Rocky? As in the sixth name John had listed? Had John known this was going to happen?*

10:00 am I sent a short text to the pastor: "What time do you get in?"

"Not till 11:00 pm. We can check in with you when we arrive."

"Please do. I think the time is drawing near."

With the advent of liquid Morphine, John's agitation and anxiety were under control, so I decided to take advantage of Trigg and Rocky at his bedside and seize the opportunity to take a shower. As good as it felt, I didn't linger. Clothed in my housecoat, I was brushing my teeth when Trigg called through the closed door.

"How soon will you be through?"

It's amazing how many thoughts can go through your mind in a matter of seconds. But foremost was the question, "Is this it?"

"Why?"

Rocky's voice responded, "John just went to Paradise."

The waiting was over and that long expected moment had arrived. In that instant, my life changed, but so did John's. Like a robot, I turned from the sink and moved my body to his bedside, emitting noises I was unaware I could make. Leaning over, I kissed him and then collapsed on his chest, wails filling the room. Even though this day had loomed large for three years, it hit me right in my heart, causing acute pain in my upper body. *Am I having a heart attack?* Trigg and Rocky had given me privacy for my grief. Time stood still as my ear rested on his soundless chest. The silence from his body was deafening.

May 26, 2015 – 11:20 am – An angel came to our bedroom and carried John to Heaven where he was greeted by Jesus, who gathered him into His arms and said, "Well done, thou good and faithful servant."

CHAPTER THIRTY-THREE

I removed the wedding ring from my husband's lifeless finger and clenched it in my hand. Even as I sat there, I mentally made plans to purchase a durable chain to wear around my neck on which to place both our rings. I removed mine and slipped it inside the circle of his. It fit perfectly, just as we had. Blinded by my tears and with our rings clasped in my hand, I held them to my breast.

As I sat beside his body, awaiting the arrival of someone to pronounce him, I felt drained of life too. He was my other half. Now what?

I sent a quick text to Pastor Phil.

"John just graduated."

"The arms of Jesus is a very good place. We will see him soon."

His reply is forever etched in my heart. Such comfort. John had traveled to Paradise and was being held. I could let him go. Sure. Like that was easy.

Feeling detached from reality, I began the task of making phone calls. My words seemed to come from someone else. *How can I actually tell someone John has died? I can't make that be true.* I remember saying, "This is that phone call." The recipient immediately knew what my reference meant. By rote, I chronicled the events of the morning. With each repetition, my words were forcing my mind to accept it as truth, but my heart still said no. His body remained motionless on the bed.

Lorri sent him one last text: "Miss you Dad. Heaven must be amazing. Love you. Your daughter."

As soon as my phone call with Tammi ended, she contacted the airlines and made arrangements to fly to my side the next day to help in whatever way she could. One of the last instructions John had given Lorri was for her to finish her school year, so it would be a few more days before she arrived.

Rocky had followed directions and called Hospice immediately. His duties completed, he quietly left. In the matter of hours I had known him, we had bonded in an unbelievable way. Now we were in a waiting game for someone to come out and verify John was deceased. The word deceased and John just wouldn't go together in my mind; it was so final.

I never left his side.

My responsibility had shifted from caretaker to decision making. Information needed to be disseminated, plans for his service completed. I was a widow. That word didn't fit me, but my new normal had arrived.

Around 1:00 pm a nurse from Hospice came. I wasn't clear on what evaluation she used to determine his death, but she agreed he was deceased. "I'll call the funeral home as soon as I leave here. They will be in touch with you regarding picking up his body." Referring to him as a body only added to my pain. He was my beloved and had a name.

Close friends began to gather, and their presence comforted my soul. No words were needed. And still I waited.

Several hours passed before two employees arrived from the funeral home. I felt I was watching a movie, and I wanted it to stop. But where was the pause button? That gurney they were bringing down the hall could not be for my husband, could it? Everything within me cried no. They positioned it beside his bed, one standing at each end, and then hesitated. Looking at me, I was asked, "Do you want to leave the room while we do this?" Tyson had returned and stood on one side of me, Trigg on the other.

"No. I want to remain right here."

They gently placed John on a cover atop the gurney and began to envelop his body with it. As they proceeded to wrap him up, one man laid a corner of it over John's face.

"He's claustrophobic."

His hand jerked back as he dropped the material. He turned to look at me with a question in his eyes. Now what?

"I'm sorry. He is, but it's okay. Go ahead." In my mind I knew John was dead, so it really didn't matter, but that reality was still disconnected from my heart. He never wanted his face covered.

They continued working until his body was entirely encased. When that was completed to their satisfaction, they rolled the gurney from the bedroom. The three of us followed them down the hall and through the front door. As John's body crossed the threshold, I thought, *he's leaving our home for the last time*. I glanced at the driveway, expecting to see a hearse, but a white station wagon sat in that spot. A station wagon? Why? As I walked behind them to the vehicle, I asked, "Why didn't you bring a hearse?"

"When we go into a neighborhood to pick up a body (there it was again…body) we don't use the hearse. It makes people in the houses uncomfortable to see one."

It seemed dishonoring to me to stick John in the back of a station wagon. Yet again, I realized John didn't care. I stood, motionless, until they turned a corner and disappeared. My husband no longer lived here.

Back inside, a flurry of activity commenced. Tyson took care of removing all signs of John's medicines, etc. carrying everything to the garage for me to deal with later. He called a friend who owned a carpet cleaning business and asked how quickly he could come out. Arrangements were made for the next morning.

Trigg helped me with the cleaning of the bedroom. The windows and shades had remained closed for days, so we threw them open for fresh air. The bed was stripped, removing everything down to the mattress. The sheets did not belong to me, so they would have to be washed and returned. The pillows and covers he had used were carried to the garage and disposed of in the trash can. Yet the air still reeked with the odor of death.

Someone from Bellevue Healthcare came to pick up his bed, bed rails, mattress, trapeze, bedside commode, wheelchair, shower chair and my bed. The young man who had been sent was given orders to pick up only John's stuff listed on an invoice in his hand. At first, he refused to take my bed because it wasn't on his orders. I had paid for it personally and it would be a separate pick up when he returned to the store. After I showed him my invoice, he finally accepted that he might as well take it too.

And now I had no bed.

Since Tyson was relieved of his duties, we shared hugs and tears before he left. He had been a solid rock for me, a constant by my side. I was so grateful for his presence during the worst days of my life. And I knew if I needed him again, he would be here. One by one, others had said their goodbyes, but Trigg was still with me.

The rest of the evening is a blank. I asked Trigg where I slept. She told me she offered me the bed in the guest bedroom, but I chose to sleep on the couch in the TV room. Looking back on that decision, I believe I felt the closest to John in there. It was where he sat each evening as he relaxed after a long day of work and where we had spent many nights during his illness with him in his chair and me on the loveseat.

When I laid down that night, my mind relocated to oblivion. Everything within me shut down allowing me to recharge.

CHAPTER THIRTY-FOUR

E arly the next morning I was getting dressed for the day when my cell phone rang. The ID said Dr. Markle.

"Hello."

"I'm sorry about John. He was a good man."

"How do you know already?"

"I read the coroner's report every morning."

"Thanks so much for calling. I really appreciate it. You took such good care of him."

Even though Phil and Anita had arrived home very late the previous evening, visiting me was the first item on their agenda. Once again, their caring hearts shone through. I knew my loss was being lifted to God through their prayers. The awareness of the depth of the bond between us was so comforting.

Dan, of Dan's Carpet Cleaning Service, arrived soon. "Tyson is a good friend. After he explained to me what happened, I agreed to do it myself. No charge." When the cleaning was complete, the overwhelming odor had been eradicated. By evening, I would have a bed again. The word had already gotten out and a Starbucks crew was ready to assemble it. The support of such wonderful friends buoyed my spirits. If I had a need, it would be met. The thoughts of facing Day One in the rest of my life without my beloved were daunting. Yet, peace that passes understanding still filled my being.

During a phone call with Lorri, I shared it had thundered after John passed away. Her response, "Well, that's a rare occurrence in eastern Washington. Of course, we know it wasn't thunder, but Dad riding the new motorcycle we prayed he would receive in heaven… the white one with a big engine. Hope he enjoys his next adventure. I sure miss him."

It was time to finalize the arrangements for John's graduation party. I called Brenda, the church secretary. After looking at the calendar, she put us down for June 6th at 11:00 am. That date was very appropriate as our local high schools were holding their graduations that day. It was suggested the military portion would be at the end, outside, as people were leaving. I immediately vetoed that. John and I desired that when people left, they would feel inspired and uplifted. The playing of taps and folding of flag would bring tears to everyone's eyes. So, it was decided we would gather outside thirty minutes ahead of time, then enter the church for the party.

So many things to take care of. Decorations. Three picture boards. A video with praise songs. A registration book. And the final information to the funeral home for the party brochure by the first of next week. The honorary pallbearers would be listed, those six names John had dictated to me days before his death, which included the name Rocky. My mind couldn't quite grasp that he knew ahead of time Rocky would be at his side when he breathed his last.

It was time to write the obituary for the newspaper. I stared at the fill-in-the-blanks form online from the TriCity Herald. It asked for John's date of birth, date of death, his parent's names, etc. I paused. Those answers told no one who John was. I closed that file, opened Word…and began to compose a picture of John. This is what I submitted.

The highway was his playground. He rode his sleek, yellow motorcycle through the twisties on Dooley Mountain…turned around and split the air curve after curve going the other way. He experienced the top of Bear Tooth Mountain in July, with snow on the roadside. He survived a night in a tent in Gillette, Wyoming with the wind, hail and rain so severe motorcycles were on their side the next morning.

He did it all with a huge grin on his face.

We traveled through Europe by train for a month with a backpack bouncing on our backs. We walked on a glacier in the ice fields of Canada and lived on a paddleboat for a week as we wound our way up the Mississippi. Boston became a favorite place to visit, and we love San Antonio.

He lived a full life.

He had many passions. It's hard to understand how making teeth could be one. It filled him with delight to give someone a beautiful smile. And of course, he had to stay on the cutting edge of technology. iPads...iPhones...Smart TV...with 3D capability.

But he loved people.

He became a part of what he called his "Starbucks Gang". When he was too weak to travel to Starbucks, they came to him, telling their tales and bringing a smile to his face. And one special angel just lived at our house, soothing him by the hour. His motorcycle buddies were very special to him. More smiles when they were together. Neighbors brought food. Friends from church gathered round to support him on his journey, some becoming nursemaid and caretaker.

It took a village...and we had one.

When the word cancer entered our world, it began to destroy John's body, but could not touch his spirit. His desire was that his cancer journey not be wasted; that others would see Jesus shining through. He gave his treatment and outcome to God.

He didn't quite make it to his anniversary...35 years of marriage to Joy Bach on June 1. This marriage created a blended family of four daughters: Tammi Reed and husband Jim, Lorri Bach, Kerri Reed and Kelly Burkhardt. In addition, a brother, Jim and wife Sam, and five grandchildren round out the family picture: Alun Greyson, Matthew Reed, Austin, McKenna and Gavin Breen.

John graduated from this earthly school on May 26, 2015. His three-year cancer journey was complete. His graduation party will be held on June 6, 2015 at 10:30 am at South Hills Church. He wanted me to specify the dress code is casual...no suits.

In John's written instructions regarding his service, he had specified no viewing, unless I felt it was necessary. It seemed it was. Our granddaughter in Seattle was adamant she needed to see him one last time; she had a letter to read to him. I contacted the funeral home and a viewing was scheduled for Saturday evening, May 30th, from 4:00-6:00 for those I invited. An unusual expense was $300 for the box he would be placed in, since there was no casket. A recommendation which surprised me was that I purchase several certified death certificates at $5 each. I bought five.

My next job was going through photos to use at the service. My eyes filled with tears as I found special pictures of John. But there was also laughter. When he experimented with bubble bath in the Jacuzzi tub, the bubbles had risen to his chin. I snapped a picture. He said, and I quote, "Okay, but don't ever let anyone see that." I set it aside for a picture board.

Tammi came on the 28th. Her husband, Jim, was scheduled for hip surgery so was unable to join us. But upon her arrival, she hit the ground running. Blessed with such a creative mind and visualization, she immediately began working on the picture boards. She and my friend, Cheryl, took over decorating the church auditorium, with special instructions for me.

"Relax. Take a bubble bath. Read a book. Let us take care of the decorations."

I did. What luxury. I read as I soaked in the warm water. It had been months since I had taken that kind of time for me. I dealt with occasional feelings of guilt but knew I had been on overload for too long, so mostly reveled in the chance to unwind.

The next day Tammi needed some additional party decorations, so we went shopping. When we returned, we entered the house through the garage, with me pausing in the kitchen. I heard her say from the living room, "Mom, you may not want to come in here." Of course, I immediately did.

The center section of our leather couch had been decimated. Pieces of the inner cushion material and leather lay all over the floor. I could see the remaining leather was not enough to have covered that portion of the couch, which could only mean Charlie had eaten it. What a mess. He was demonstrating his grief in a very visual way. We loved on him, but from that day forward, he was relegated to the laundry room or outside when we left the house. He never got sick from his unusual diet.

The texts and cards continued to arrive. One from a motorcycle rider friend: "Joy, I hope you are surrounded with family and friends. Our hearts are with you." Love was pouring in from every direction.

I purchased a ticket for our granddaughter to fly here from Seattle so she could see grandpa one last time. When the two-hour time slot for the viewing ended, she wouldn't leave. Her distress was hard on me, so I left Tammi to deal with her and I went to the car. I had planned to take them out to eat afterward but could see that wasn't an option. I suggested we all go have a strawberry milkshake, since that was the only thing John could eat toward the end. It was a good choice. Soon we were sharing stories about him as we sucked on the straws.

John had left typed instructions about his wishes for the service:

NO CASKET
No viewing, except for family members at a different time, if they so choose. (Unless you feel it is necessary)
   I do not want a funeral. **I want a graduation party.**
   Pastor Phil: No suits
   Here are the songs:
      You're Number One by the Gatlin Brothers (with words on the screen)
      It is Well With My Soul (with words on the screen)
      I'll Praise You in This Storm – sung by Tyson Pischel, Dean Durham and Steve Linn
      Amazing Grace – sung by Phil Driscoll
      I Then Shall Live – Gaither's song – sung by Tyson, Dean and Steve
   Favorite scripture: 1st John 4:7-12

On June 1st, to celebrate our anniversary, I went to Outback, ate a steak, baked potato and scraped the bottom of the bowl that held the complimentary ice cream sundae. John and I began our married life on June 1, 1980, and what a wonderful 35-year chapter it had been. But now I have a confession to make. Most of the days after his passing are a blur. I'm not sure who I went out to eat with, other than Tammi. I do know I was determined to think happy thoughts and share good memories, but probably leaked a tear or two.

On June 2nd, several of us met at the church to discuss the service. Tyson volunteered to take care of the video with pictures and music, plus talking to Dean and Steve regarding singing. I requested one song to be sung by Debi Eng. John loved her singing, and I loved the words of the song All My Tears. No one had heard of it, including Debi, who learned it in two days. Serving cookies and drink was suggested, but I asked that food be served. The people attending would be friends who had been present at various parties in our home, and we always served food. Once again, volunteers stepped up and would provide an ample meal.

By the 5th, family had begun to arrive. Lorri's school year was finally over, and she was on the next flight here. It had been hard on her to postpone joining us. John's daughter Kelly and her children from Boise, Idaho, his brother Jim from Henderson, Nevada, his nephew Walter from Blackfoot, Idaho, and cousin Bill from Boise all came. A very close friend and sometimes business partner, Barry Treasure, drove in from Idaho Falls, Idaho.

This was real. It was happening. They were gathering to say the final goodbye. Somehow my heart and mind could not get in sync with that fact.

CHAPTER THIRTY-FIVE

It's a strange feeling to wake up and know this is the day…the day we would gather to share funny stories and shed some tears as we said our goodbyes to John. I felt the love and support from my daughters when I wandered into the kitchen. I was very aware I would experience varied emotions as the day transpired…laughter and crying…all mingled with my deep love for him.

Soon it was time to get dressed.

I glanced at my clothes in the closet, but already knew what I would be wearing. Weeks before, John had stood beside me as he pointed to his choice of jacket for me to wear to his party. "That's my favorite. And I think it goes well with jeans." It was a Coldwater Creek jacket we had purchased in Seattle, on one of our weekend getaways. He had discovered it on a rack and excitedly shown it to me.

Enough said.

The decorations were amazing. His BMW t-shirts and sweatshirts hung from a clothesline. A round table with the Starbucks logo had been borrowed and various Starbucks drink containers were displayed there. A large picture of John graced the front of the room, surrounded by beautiful flower arrangements. Each table was covered in a bright yellow tablecloth and had an assortment of helium filled graduation balloons tied to Propel bottles, his drink of choice. Tent cards stating one of his recent sayings were on the tables: **Enjoy life. It has an expiration date!** Small favors were at each place, comprised of a black stand, golden rolled up diploma and cap with tassel on top. In the small space under the cap was a picture of John.

First it was time to gather outside the church for the military portion. Tyson had been told the people doing the ceremony didn't have a trumpet player, so Taps would be a recording. Not good enough. He enlisted one of our church members, Jim Jamison, to play. That's when the tears began. Next was the folding of the flag segment. Two members of the military stood in front of me facing each other. They reached for the corners of the flag and with a loud snap, it opened completely. Then they slowly and precisely folded the triangles, smoothing all wrinkles out, until the ends were tucked in and they could hand it to me. I hugged it as I tried valiantly to curb my sobs. Then came the 21-gun salute.

I held it together, barely.

The atmosphere changed when we entered the auditorium. Praise music and the sound of our friends greeting each other filled the air. Pastor Phil stood in front, wearing shorts and a polo shirt. With a grin he explained, "In forty years of conducting funerals, I have never dressed this way. John gave me explicit instructions on what to wear."

For sharing time, I took the mic. "Several people have asked me how John and I met. So here's the story. I grew up controlled by fear of God and everything else. In my legalistic world I never stepped outside the church cocoon. While we were still in high school, my first marriage was arranged by my mother and the church. I was barely thirty years old when that union ended. That's when I began a journey of discovery about the world outside the church. Imagine my surprise to learn that what I had been taught about God was not true. I worked on sorting my beliefs for months. I told God two things. "If you want me to get married again, you're going to have to plant him right in front of me and I am through saying no to experiences out of fear."

One weekend my children were out of town visiting their father. Friends had invited me to join them at their church. I have no idea what the sermon was about, because I felt God telling me to speak to that pastor, a man I had never met, and volunteer my services to help him get a singles group started. *Why had I told God I wouldn't say no to experiences out of fear?* My heart was pounding out of my chest and my face was beet red as I walked up to him after church and offered my help. That's how I ended up the next Saturday morning sitting in the outer office of that pastor. In came a man dressed in tank top and shorts, all sweaty, (having jogged to the church) and sat down beside me. I moved away just a little. The pastor came out and called us into his office. We were there to discuss how to get the singles group started. That man's name was John and God had planted him right in front of me. Seven years after my divorce, I married again."

Jim, John's brother, spoke of their childhood and ended by saying. "A few months ago, John traveled to my home in Nevada. We both knew it was a time of goodbye. But he also wanted to make sure I knew Jesus and he would see me again."

Then the stories began. Hilarious ones. Tender ones. Starbucks stories. Motorcycle stories. Interspersed with those were stories of how John had shared about his cancer journey and God's love. Some I had heard before. Others amazed me as I listened. John had become very bold as he lived with a terminal illness.

Pastor Phil shared stories of our life. One that brought laughter was when he explained John had learned how to placate me when we didn't agree. "He would tell her, "You may be right" and then they would laugh, as both understood what John was doing."

I watched a slideshow, listened to our friends as they sang, and then another slideshow began on the screen. From the very first strains of the song, my dam broke. There were so many memories imbedded in "We're Number One" by Larry Gatlin and the Gatlin Brothers. The song had been new to me when I met John. It became our song.

The words so clearly depicted our lives. Shattered. Scattered pieces. Putting them back together was hard. But we vowed our love would find a way. Those who knew us well said it could never be done. Our nine-month separation three years after our marriage almost proved them right. We emerged from that time entwined as one unit and our love forged an unbreakable bond. John carried that CD in his car and when we traveled, he would play it on repeat. We memorized the words and pointed to each other as we sang "you'd be number one". Hearing our intimate words was my undoing.

Thus, the flood from my eyes.

The party concluded with an invitation to partake from the overwhelming bounty of food awaiting on tables in the hallway. Volunteers had provided a wonderful variety of dishes. People ate and ate, commenting on how fantastic everything was. And then there was dessert...lots of it...complete with a cake that read "Congratulations Graduate!"

The party had been exactly as John envisioned.

Several families who attended were leaving to join in other graduation celebrations. Their high school students were graduating that afternoon to be followed by parties at their homes. I offered them all our decorations and they divided them up into various cars. It felt good to know we had contributed to their festivities.

When Charlie damaged our couch, he had destroyed only the center section. We now had that portion covered with a quilt. The end sections were still usable. As the family gathered at our home, we shared Charlie's story, which led to more narratives of past pets...and then antics of the humans involved.

John and Jim had grown up around Walter. It was delightful to hear the tales of their childhood and we could feel John's presence. As evening approached, friends provided a delicious meal, and more food was consumed. All too soon it was time for another round of goodbyes, as planes needed to be boarded and cars driven many miles the next day.

We had truly honored John this day.

Tammi was next to leave. She had been with me ten days but needed to get home, since her husband was scheduled for surgery. She had taken such a burden from my shoulders with her preparations, organizing and making sure I ate. Oh, how I appreciated her caring heart during these first days of transition. Saying goodbye to her was hard.

Now I was one step closer to my new life of living alone.

CHAPTER THIRTY-SIX

Lorri and I had a few days left before she returned to Georgia. One of John's favorite places to eat was the Ice-Burg Drive-In in Walla Walla, so we decided to go there. Charlie excitedly jumped in the car when we invited him along. We ordered at the window and walked to the area where there were two tables. One was already occupied by what looked like a grandma, mom and dad, and a little girl. She immediately spied Charlie and asked if she could pet him. His tail was already thumping a welcome. Then she looked at the bench beside me and asked, "Who's that man with you?" Every hair on my head stood up. *Was John with us?* Lorri and I stared at each other…wordless. Assured by her parents no one was there, she was adamant. "He looks like a nice man."

All too soon, it was Lorri who walked through the security line and out of sight at the airport. Before she disappeared, she turned for one last wave. Our goodbye hug had been packed with deep emotion. Just two months previously, John had risen from his wheelchair to stand beside her in a courtroom, declaring her his daughter.

Tears streamed down my face as I headed for my car. When I arrived home, I would be living alone for the first time in my seventy-two years. During my childhood I had lived with my mother who handed me off to a husband. When that marriage ended, I had three children at home. Seven years later, with two daughters still living with me, I married John. He and I had talked about what my challenges might be as a widow, a word I couldn't associate with me. Today, I faced that reality. What a formidable thought. My car became a refuge as God's presence flooded every nook and cranny, assuring me He would be right beside me as I traversed this unfamiliar path.

With His help, my emotions stabilized enough for me to drive.

More robot than human, I moved through the motions of putting the house in order, though there wasn't much to do. My family and friends had taken care of what they could. As I picked up papers and sorted through them, I decided to put some in a special place for safe keeping. When I opened the container, a folded sheet of paper lay on top. Curious, I picked it up and unfolded it. The word at the top of the page instantly destabilized those emotions I thought I had under control.

"Flesh".

That was the private word John and I used for each other. I dropped to the floor as I realized these were John's words to me. I read a sentence and sobbed. One more sentence. More sobbing. It seemed he was right beside me.

Flesh,

Although my body is gone, I am still very much with you in spirit. I always admired your strength, and I left this earth knowing that you would remain strong, regardless of the depth of your grief. You will keep your head up and move forward.

Thank you for believing in me when I didn't believe in myself. Your steadfast patience is extraordinary, and you truly demonstrated the concept of unconditional love. You made me want to be a better man, a better father, a better husband, a better friend.

In the end, even as cancer ravaged my body, you were my rock. How I wish I could have spared you the pain of caring for someone who couldn't care for himself. I know it broke your heart to witness my struggle, yet you didn't fall apart. You are remarkable.

My graduation party was just as I had envisioned it. It was such an honor to see my family and friends gathered together, with Pastor Phil in his shorts… My spirit smiled. ☺

I am with you when you walk through our house, still processing the idea that I won't come home. I see you as your eyes linger on my chair, as your hand reaches out to touch me in our bed, and as you sit at our dining room table, remembering the mornings we sat together to pray, talk, and spend time together.

I see you when you sit on the patio, enjoying the evening breeze, contemplating the new life that you didn't ask for. I see you when you look into Charlie's eyes, unable to explain why I won't walk through the door.

Our love story isn't over, as I am with you always...
Someday, we will be together again...
You're still number one...
I love you...
John

My sobbing subsided. I wasn't alone. Jesus and John were with me. I could make it.

Father's Day was coming up and time for the annual weekend motorcycle rally in John Day, Oregon which we had attended every year with friends from our area. Hundreds of people from all over the United States and a few from other countries would congregate at the Fair Grounds. I always drove my car, loaded with all the extras that wouldn't fit on their motorcycles. I was the mule. Plans had been made to use me again this year. But this would be the first year I would stay in a motel, not in a tent. Apparently, John had given the tent away. Motel rooms needed to be reserved a year in advance, and my discovery had been only a few days previously. But when the gang heard about my dilemma, one couple volunteered their motel room to me, and they slept in a tent.

Saturday morning, we gathered at our group's area. The agenda was to take John's ashes to the top of his favorite ride, Dooley Mountain, and assemble there for a little ceremony. The chance for me to ride on the back of one of the motorcycles was extended, but I voted no. My reason, it's a very technical bit of twisties rising to over four thousand feet, containing one hundred seventy curves in fifteen miles. No way would I hang on to someone for that ride. Not even for John.

About twenty riders gathered for group pictures and then I videotaped their departure. My thoughts were with them as I crocheted and read in my lawn chair. For lunch, I walked to my favorite restaurant, The Outpost, and enjoyed a Mexican pizza.

I hugged the riders as they began to straggle in. Eating was the first order of the evening, so they went their various ways. By 7:00

pm all had returned. They shared about the time spent at the top of Dooley, words that were spoken and prayers given. And then it was time for a toast to John. His favorite beer, Deschutes Black Butte, had been purchased. Each of us was given a small Dixie cup with that foul smelling stuff in it. Several toasts were given. I raised my cup and said, "Only for you, John, would I take one swallow." It was awful, but I had saluted him.

Driving was always such good therapy. I played a memories tape in my head as I covered the miles heading home. My life had forever changed, but my friends were still there.

The week unfolded before me. On my to-do list was buy a ring engraved with the words "Always and Forever" to wear with my wedding ring. After shopping at several nice jewelry stores, I had not found one who could do that. They all recommended Walmart. Walmart? But sure enough, I placed an order and would receive it in a few days. My kids had given me a gift certificate to a spa, so I spent several hours treating myself to a massage and pedicure. Trigg came over that evening. We worked on a puzzle while we talked and then finished off with a pizza.

Life was different, but still good.

As I headed for bed, I talked to God. *Thank you for a good day...for your presence. I feel blessed to know I have you, my friends, my health, my wonderful home and enough money to pay my bills. I look forward to a good night's sleep.*

John had asked me what the hardest thing would be for me after he was gone. It took no thought to answer him. "Going to bed. We always snuggle and spoon, hold hands and reach for each other in the night. I'm going to fall out of bed looking for you." We prayed I would be able to sleep soundly and wake up refreshed. From the very first night, that prayer had been answered. I laid down at bedtime and awoke rested each morning.

CHAPTER THIRTY-SEVEN

O ne of the first orders of my new life was to generate a modified will. The finality of John's death hit me again as I spoke with our lawyer. There was no future "us" in the legal issues. My revisions were approved. I then drove from my lawyer's office to meet with another friend, a Realtor. It was now up to me to sell the building that had housed our business. Gratitude flooded me as I comprehended the magnitude of my reliance on my village. Whatever questions I faced, someone I trusted would be available with an answer.

My next stop was a financial advisor introduced to me by my boss. John and I had no retirement plan, but with the payout of his life insurance, I had some financial assets that would provide a little cushion. Decisions needed to be made regarding the management of those funds. At the end of the day, exhaustion overtook me. My brain felt dead, and I just wanted to stare off into space. My choices had been made and I determined there was no need for second guessing.

The days just kept happening. Some were better than others. Most of the time I felt emotionless, like a robot. Other days I felt the need to go through some more of his things. I hadn't been able to open John's wallet, so had laid it on my desk. I felt brave enough to try again.

The brown leather billfold contained the essence of John.

The first thing I noticed was what he had written on the protective sleeve for his enhanced driver's license. *John 3:16 1150 + 650 = fun.* That one took me awhile, then my lightbulb came on. His last two motorcycles were an 1150 and a 650. He was a Christian who rode motorcycles and had fun.

As I continued my perusal, I could feel John's presence. His wallet had gone with him everywhere, including numerous hospital rooms. He left it in my protection as he underwent tests, therapies, and surgeries. His identity was contained in that wallet. As I sorted through his things, a sobering thought hit me. I couldn't carry what truly mattered in my purse or John in his wallet. His love of God and people did not reside in his pocket, but inhabited his heart, one full of love.

I placed his wallet on a shelf in my new office, one I had not painted pink.

During our marriage, we had taken a lot of trips together. This time he had gone on a journey without me. I lived in limbo.

It had been good advice to buy some death certificates. They now came into play. I tried removing John's name from our internet provider. First one person and then another explained to me I couldn't just call and do that, then they transferred me to someone else. It seemed my only option was to get in the car and drive to their office. Once they held the death certificate in their hands, I was allowed to remove his name. Several other companies treated me the same way.

My worst encounter came at the credit union. John had a small account there under just his name. The young lady at the counter ushered me into a room with the admonition, "Just wait right here. I'll see if I can find someone to help you." So, I waited. Finally, a man entered and I had to repeat my whole story again. Tears were threatening. It was so hard to keep telling people that John had died. I had the death certificate in my hand. Why couldn't they just believe it? After hearing my information, he acknowledged he didn't have the authority to take care of my problem and proceeded to call Seattle.

The phone was handed to me. I was told, "His funds cannot be released without his signature." I was beyond being polite. "He's dead. That's going to be hard to do." I was placed on hold. Another voice came over the phone. "Could you please explain to me what it is you are trying to do?" In the end, no one believed me that John could not sign anything. HE WAS DEAD! But without his signature, the funds would not be released.

I made it to the car before I broke down. It was hard enough for me to carry John's death certificate to various places, without them arguing with me they needed his signature. Pain and anger boiled within me. I wanted to lash out…break their windows…or something. They had inflicted unnecessary anguish on me, and it seemed they didn't care. Overwhelming annoyance was an unusual emotion for me, and I dealt with it for quite some time as I sat in my car. I knew it wasn't safe for me to drive. As a NASCAR fan, I was ready to do "bump and runs" on anyone who got in my way.

I finally calmed down enough to go home. But it was days before my resentment subsided. With God's help, I let go of the desire for retribution. I was only hurting myself by playing it over and over in my head and I needed my energy for this new life I was living. But over the following months I did monitor John's account. A $5 fee was billed each month until the funds disappeared.

July 3rd was approaching…John's 69th birthday. I took myself to Outback, taking one of the favors to set on the table. Even though there was a three-hour time difference between Lorri and me, she was seated at Outback too, doing the same. We sang happy birthday over the phone.

It was time for another party, this time complete with a birthday cake for John. Forty people came to celebrate. Happy birthday was sung, with my boss saying, "I guess we shouldn't add that part about "and many more" should we?" Laughter, a wonderful sound in my home.

As the fog in my mind lessened, I caught myself talking with God a lot. *So why did you allow John to die?* "You're not asking the right question. Ask what I want to teach you; what I want to do with your life now."

That led me to a pen and notebook. I sat in the swing on the patio and emptied my thoughts onto paper. *What is my purpose now? What does God want me to do? I'm trying to figure out His Plan B for my life.*

More insights from God. "I don't have a Plan B. This is all still part of Plan A."

When those words registered, everything seemed to fall into place. All through his illness, John and I had agreed either way was okay. God could heal him here on earth and we would continue with our life, or God could heal him in Heaven where he would never be sick again. If it was God's plan to heal him in Heaven, then he had a plan for me too here on earth. I just had to understand what that was.

Life was returning to a semblance of normalcy. Twenty-five people attended my fall party. Within days I was packed and ready to fly to California to a DLOBA meeting. John had asked that a portion of his ashes be scattered in the ocean. Friends in DLOBA were going to help make that happen. But those plans encountered some difficulties. At the airport, as my carry-on bag went through the machine, it was removed from the belt. The man behind the counter approached me and asked, "Do you have human remains in this bag?" Who knew they could tell that? Instantly, I had visions of them throwing John in some trash can. My tears were not fake as I shared what my intentions were. He allowed me to keep John.

The next evening Tammi and Jim came from Pasadena to join with our group for dinner at McCormick & Schmick's in Irvine, California. They had been with DLOBA before and knew several members. During the following day we enjoyed some family time as I didn't attend the meetings. That evening our group was scheduled to board the Hornblower Yacht *Endless Dreams* at 6:00 pm for a Newport Beach dinner cruise. Again, we had plans for John's ashes. Once we got out into the water, we would have a little ceremony and scatter them on the ocean. A photographer arrived to take a group picture before we boarded. One of my friends yelled, "Hey, Joy. Where's John?" "In a bag in my pocket." "He wants to be in the picture too. Get him out." I was placed in the middle of the front row, holding a little baggie.

The photographer heard all that. She asked me, "What do you have in that bag?" Many answers flew through my head. While I was deciding which one to pick, she asked, "Are those human remains?" Once again, I wondered what was going to become of John. When I responded yes, she said nothing more.

Aboard the yacht, seated at the tables awaiting our delectable dinner, I saw the Captain coming toward me. "I think I'm about to be called to the principal's office." Sure enough. He squatted beside me and said, "You are not allowed to scatter ashes in these waters. I just want you to know I'll be watching you." I smiled at him and said, "Okay" as in my mind I sang, *Every move you make, every step you take, I'll be watching you.* John remained in my pocket. Some friends volunteered to do it anyway, but I said no. I wasn't sure what the consequences would be.

At breakfast new plans were made. Since the meeting was official-ly over, several members were leaving. But two wonderful friends sat across from us and shared they would surfboard out into the ocean and scatter the ashes for me. Before they did that, we would conduct a little ceremony on the beach. Tammi and Jim took me to the designated spot, but even though I had prepared words in my head, they refused to come out. I listened as others spoke of love and caring, promise and peace. Then the volunteers picked up their surfboards and headed out. For one, it was his first time on a board. Such love.

I had fulfilled one more of John's wishes.

CHAPTER THIRTY-EIGHT

One week later, I sat on the floor and leaned back against the recliner. That quickly Charlie was by my side with his head in my lap. Tears were flowing. I had just finalized arrangements for a wonderful trip to Israel joining Paul Null in his tour group, fulfilling a long-held desire. But I would be traveling without John. That just didn't seem right. I longed to share my experiences with him, and so I grieved.

I didn't fall apart. I dried my tears, got up, gathered my purse and car keys, and headed out the door to go to lunch with Carol, a dear friend. We would talk and laugh, I might shed another tear or two, and would probably eat too much. It was all part of the grieving process.

I continued the pattern of giving parties. Every four months, friends gathered in my home, anywhere from twenty-five to forty-two in attendance. We could always feel John with us, but it never dampened the atmosphere. He wouldn't want us moping around.

I was still finding little surprises from him. One day I found a handwritten note on a piece of torn off yellow legal pad.

What you did for me.
Gave me motorcycle rides without guilt
Cooked me roast
Was my best friend
Became my pharmacist's assistant
Proofed my emails
Gave me laughter

Simple things like going to Costco or to the grocery store remained difficult. John really enjoyed Costco. When I asked him what he needed that caused him to go there so often, he explained, "You don't know what you need until you get there." He loved it when I agreed our Friday night date could be a trip to Costco. My first trip there without him, I discovered it was way too hard. I left the cart where it was and walked out. Going to the grocery store triggered the same effect. I had been buying groceries with him in mind for thirty-five years. I would reach for something I knew he liked, and then jerk my hand back, remembering he had no need for it.

I now used what had been his office. One day, sitting in his chair as I read the Bible placed on the desk in front of me, I came across a passage I felt needed clarification. I wondered if one of my older Bibles had some of my notes in the margin to help me understand it better. When I reached for a Bible on the shelf above the desk, it slipped in my hand and I almost dropped it. Pages fluttered and a piece of paper fell out. Instantly I recognized the handwriting. Tentatively I picked up the note, my breath on pause. Before I could read two words, tears streamed down my face.

Thank you for loving me in so many practile ways
like hamburger gravy and cottage cheese
Flesh

I experienced a full-blown meltdown.

Sometimes I could go for days without the intense sense of missing my beloved. At other times, it seemed I couldn't shake off the longing to see him again, touch his hand, hear his voice…to connect in some way. God knew what I needed, so He provided. Here it was, in John's handwriting, his expression of love for me. In that moment it felt like he was right there in the room with me. I basked in the love of God and John. I wasn't alone.

Who knew when he had placed that note in my Bible? And as I'm sure you noticed; he wasn't the world's best speller.

One morning I sat in the swing on the shaded patio, enjoying the breeze and the early morning bird songs, the sun peeking through the trees. A gorgeous day was at hand. *We built such a lovely house, designed for our old age; all on one floor, wide halls and low maintenance. John only got to enjoy it for two years before his diagnosis. What a shame he can't delight in the home he put so much thought into.*

Just that quickly, a new awareness hit. *Duh. He's living in a mansion and isn't missing this house at all. I guess it's up to me to enjoy it, and so I will.*

I had wondered if I could ever get to the place of feeling whole again. Oh, don't take me wrong. I was living a wonderful life. Friends. Family. Travel. But "whole" was so much deeper than those things. I had been numb, moving through my days like a robot. Half of me was missing. I was no longer the same person. But who was I? As the weeks and months passed, my mind began to partially function again.

I knew I needed to find a purpose for my days.

In a conversation with Lorri, I told her, "I want to go see Dr. Ness one more time. He was so good with John and so gentle and caring. I sent him a thank you card, but I need to thank him in person." Her response, "I'll make cookies for you to take."

The cookies arrived and I drove the familiar route to Dr. Ness's office. So many memories. A wheelchair still waited in the foyer for that patient without enough strength to walk any further. The elevator rose to the routine floor. I walked to the counter where I was greeted warmly. One employee came around to hug me. "May I see Dr. Ness? It's not for a medical exam. I just want to thank him and give him some cookies." That message was delivered to him.

I waited, unsure if it was okay to hug your doctor. But he wasn't our doctor anymore. I vacillated. The minute Dr. Ness walked into the waiting room, I wrapped my arms around him and squeezed. He squeezed back. My thank you had been given and received.

During the second year after John's death, the frozen parts of me began to thaw. That brought pain...such pain. Yet, I knew I must go on. As a Christ-follower, I turned to Him without ceasing. *Please show me the way.*

I was very aware that everyone's grief journey is different. I read many books describing others' journeys. There were no rules. It was necessary for me to travel this path at my own speed. Each step of the way, I felt God's love holding me up.

John was my partner in everything. When he knew his life was ending, we talked about me following my passion…writing. Since our business had been called Design Dental Lab and our home-based business was Design Marketing Consultants, he had suggested when I was ready to get serious about writing that I call it Words by Design. As the days passed, I began to feel writing was my ministry. I registered for a business license – Words by Design – and through much trial and error, created a blog website, thewordsbydesign.com.

Baby steps.

Currently, I have published three books, but they were words already written on my website and for another organization called FaithWriters. There wasn't much thinking involved in placing those short stories and articles in order and then printing them. The book you are now reading was different, composed from scratch.

I was unprepared for how hard that would be. I didn't even know where to start. The jumble of words in my head were just that, a jumble of words. Normally, I don't procrastinate. Normally, I find time in my day for what matters to me. Normally, I feel I've accomplished what I set out to do. In every other area of my life that was true. But not this one.

Book four had been a pile of papers and binders, and even some notes in my husband's handwriting, items to help trigger thoughts. The whole concept of organizing those facts, thoughts and feelings and putting them in a narrative was overwhelming. For days I struggled with my lack of expertise. The book was to be about us and how we handled his cancer journey. My aspiration was that others would see how God had traveled that transition time with us, helping us believe that either way, it was okay.

I leaned heavily on the verse in Philippians 1:6 that told me, "He who began a good work in you will carry it on to completion….." I gave the book to Him. *God, you must be glorified through this.*

Slowly, I discovered a rhythm that worked for me in my new normal. God was still in control. John and I had prayed for more than his healing. Our desire had been to experience God's presence in our lives as we traveled this journey, and we had received a fuller, more satisfying outcome for our souls. My inner peace remained and I continued to sleep soundly every night. As I moved through this corridor in time, my days began to achieve balance.

Sometimes the words flowed; sometimes it was tears. As I wrote, I encountered a phenomenon new to me. I became so fully into the story I found it difficult to pull myself out and back to the current world. When it came time to write about his death, I took several weeks off. I had no idea that seven years later, those emotions would still be so intense.

These words came to me in the early hours of New Year's Day, 2022. "This book is not about goodbye – it's about hello."

John has experienced an awesome "hello" in heaven. On a regular basis my learning curve brings me to a new "hello" in my life. My hope of what will happen because of this book is that you will grasp a new "hello" in your concept of God.

Going through cancer, we discovered God is enough. John was right. Either way, it's okay.

EPILOGUE

I began working on this book about a month before the sixth anniversary of John's death. A few times over the previous years, I had tried to write this story, but the pain was just too great. I began to slowly recall our experiences; sometimes undergoing an instant meltdown and other times I would laugh out loud as I typed a funny incident. I felt very raw as I re-lived this journey.

As I wrote these words, I prayed for two types of readers, the Christian and non-Christian. If you are a Christian, you will understand how we knew without a doubt that God loved us and was walking with us through every circumstance. For those who read this and do not know Jesus, I pray you can see God's love shining through. Even though our world was falling apart, we believed God had a purpose behind His plan.

I had all the medical paraphernalia, binders with the doctor information and other items laying on a counter and table in my writing room to help trigger my memories. When I completed the first draft of 55,000 words, I believed I no longer needed those objects and decided it was time to store them away. It seemed like a good idea.

I carried some containers into the room and turned on music to listen to as I worked. The very first song that began playing was **We're Number One**. I heard the first chords and erupted in ugly crying. I felt like I was getting rid of more of him. For those traveling the grief journey, you never know when it will rise up and hit you. Tears streamed down my face as I packed the stuff away. Above me, on the wall was a plaque that says, "My marriage didn't end when I became a widow." So true.

Almost 60,000 words done, I struggled with how to end. Days went by as I avoided my writing room. I had lost my way. It was also a hard time of year with the anniversaries of his death, his graduation party, our anniversary, and his birthday. Months before, my kids and I had planned a trip to spend time together. It would be good to get away.

When we arrived and were getting settled in, Tammi and Jim went to the grocery store. That's when Lorri came into my room and said, "I have an anniversary present for you. It's kind of an unusual gift. I hope you like it." She handed me a three-inch square box. Removing the lid, a golden compass lay nestled on black velvet. The words "My Forever Love" were engraved on the top. Upon opening the compass, more words were inside. "You are my favorite adventure." I stared at it. A compass. When you are lost, a compass is a good thing to have. Immediately I felt John's love emanating from those words and I knew I could finish the book. Poor Lorri. She had no idea what was happening in my head and when I didn't speak, she had doubts about her gift.

As we talked, I assured her it was perfect and told her my side of the story. She told me she kept seeing an ad on Facebook for a compass and felt she was supposed to buy it. But why a compass? Days went by. The ad kept appearing. Finally, she purchased it, and then there were no more ads.

In my Bible reading one day after John's death, I came across a scripture that brought laughter. Oh, how I wished I could share it with him.

I Kings 1:1-4 NIV

When King David was very old, he could not keep warm even when they put covers over him. So, his attendants said to him, "Let us look for a young virgin to serve the king and take care of him. She can lie beside him so that our lord the king may keep warm." Then they searched throughout Israel for a beautiful young woman and found Abishag, a Shunmmite, and brought her to the king. The woman was very beautiful; she took care of the king and waited on him, but the king had no sexual relations with her.

You read how John was cold all the time. We didn't try this.

There are some people (and dogs) mentioned in this book who have now joined John.

Jim
Charlie
Paul
Carol
Bob (Sky's dad)
Plus, our dog, Charlie, and Trigg's dog, Vivien.

A few months ago I received word that Steve, the young man who helped scatter John's ashes in the ocean, was killed in an accident.

I've learned some lessons in my grief. I had a choice to make. I could give in to the void created by John's death…or I could still choose life and purpose.

I came to realize that others do not know what to say to me. Some say things that do not help, and others just avoid me. Then there are those who know to just be there. No words are necessary. I can't even begin to express the gratitude I have for my "village". They are there… like a rock. No matter what I need. And they are okay with my remoteness or ugly crying.

I kept trying to accept the fact I was now living Plan B. I didn't want Plan B. It took me two years to understand I am still living Plan A. There is no B. Jeremiah 29:11 – God has a plan for me. It includes this journey.

But most of all, I know I can just be held by God. When there are no words, He holds me. When I've shed buckets of tears, He holds me. When I'm depleted, He is by my side. And when I'm ready to get up and go again, He goes with me.

I do not know how human beings go through this kind of grief without Him.

John on his new bike

Tent city in John Day

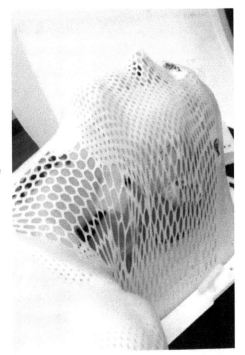

Mask screwed to table

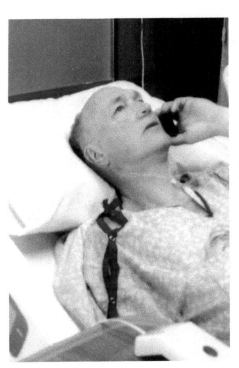

On phone with dentist

Greg Iles in Natchez

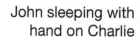
John sleeping with
hand on Charlie

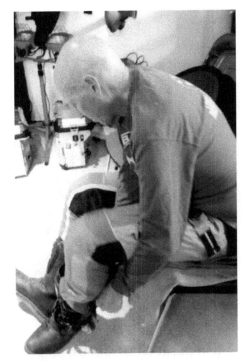

Ready for a ride after completing chemo

Red Cadillac

Standing in pontoon on the Columbia River

Graduation Party

Party cake

Group ready to ride to the top of Dooley for ceremony

Toast to John at the campground

Me holding bag of ashes in front of the Hornblower

My Dearest Memory of John

One of my dearest memories of John is a picture in my head.

He was getting ready to go on a ten-day motorcycle trip with friends. I did all I could to help him think of what he might need; snacks, a map just in case one of the men was man enough to look at it and various other items. His bike was in the garage right outside the kitchen door. When I thought he was ready, I went back inside the house.

He always held me, and we prayed before he left. So, I waited for him to come in. And I waited a few more minutes. Since this was a longer trip than usual, I thought maybe he had forgotten something else and was looking for it in the cupboards out there.

I waited some more. No John. I opened the door to the garage. There he was on his knees with a hand resting on the seat of the motorcycle.

I quietly closed the door.

MEET JOY BACH

Even though Joy is retired, she stays busy and wonders how she ever had time for work. She celebrated her 75th birthday with the publication of her first book, Life Moments with Joy. Two years later her second book was published, More Life Moments with Joy. One year later her third book came out, The Challenge. She discovered writing is her new calling.

Joy looks forward to what experiences come next in her life journey.

Many of her priorities changed during 2020. Her travels, spending time with family and going out to eat with friends came to a halt. A group she created for widows, Life after Loss, could no longer meet. But that left more time for working jigsaw puzzles, reading, and her ministry of crocheting or knitting afghans for others. A big slot of her newfound time was devoted to the birth of this book. Since the gym was closed, she had to change her exercise routine. She now has a walking loop in her house. And she became familiar with words like streaming and Google Meet.

For more of Joy's articles or to contact her, visit her website at: thewordsbydesign.com

CPSIA information can be obtained
at www.ICGtesting.com
Printed in the USA
LVHW040106250223
740097LV00004B/7